LONDO
HANDB

Capital Transport

INTRODUCTION

This book gives details of the buses working on London Transport routes and thus combines most of the information formerly included in the London Bus Handbooks Part 1 and Part 2.

The appearance of new vehicles on London's bus services continues at a high rate as many re-tendered services specify the use of new buses. The specification of red buses on routes which enter the central London zone has resulted in the first red-liveried buses for Grey-Green and Capital Citybus. New bus operator Limebourne also employs red liveried vehicles on minibus service C10.

The authors gratefully acknowledge the willing assistance of many of the operators concerned. Particular help has been given by Tony Cole, Bernie Elsom, Keith Grimes, Jef Johnson, Glyn Matthews and David Stewart, and officers of the London Omnibus Traction Society and the PSV Circle. Readers who would like further information on developments within the fleets are recommended to consult the news-sheets of the enthusiasts' societies mentioned.

January 1997   Nicholas King and Colin Lloyd

Front cover photo: Geoff Rixon
Back cover photos: Gerald Mead and Tony Wilson
Title page photo: Mark Lyons

ISBN 185414 189 9

First published 1977
Eighteenth edition 1997

Published by Capital Transport Publishing
38 Long Elmes, Harrow Weald, Middlesex

Printed by Bath Midway Press, Holt, Wiltshire

CONTENTS

ARMCHAIR

Armchair Passenger Transport Co Ltd,
Armchair House, Commerce Way, Brentford, TW8 8LZ

Armchair Passenger Transport gained LT tendered routes 260 from June 1990 and 65 from January 1991. These followed their original foray into bus operation with the acquisition of Green Line route 733, tendered at deregulation in October 1986, and a subsequent contract for routes 750 and 751, both of which have since ceased. The Company was also successful in gaining tendered work from both Royal Berkshire and Surrey County Councils.

The latest LT routes to be won are the 117 from August 1996 and route 190 from December 1996, both of which necessitated the purchase of new buses. These have taken the form of new Dennis Darts with Plaxton bodywork, which are in a revised livery with white roofs and black window surrounds and skirts.

Current LT routes operated are 65, 117, 190, 260; other routes are 441, 564, 592, 691. The fleet carries orange and white livery, and is housed at Commerce Way, Brentford.

Among the newest vehicles in the Armchair fleet are seven Plaxton Pointer bodied Dennis Darts. Allocated to tendered route 117, they operate between Isleworth and Staines. P28MLE was photographed in September 1996 in Hounslow High Street. Malc McDonald

The latest addition to the Armchair double deck fleet is this former Rhondda Leyland Olympian with Eastern Coach Works body acquired in 1995. Richmond Bus Station provides the setting for MUH289X in July 1996. Mike Harris

One of a trio of Roe bodied Leyland Atlanteans purchased second hand from South Yorkshire in 1990, GIL2605 is seen here in Queen Elizabeth Road, Kingston during July. The type is normally to be found on route 65 covering for the standard Leyland Olympians. Geoff Rixon

A one-off in the Armchair fleet is this Wadham Stringer bodied Leyland Swift, seen at Staines in August 1996. Richard Godfrey

ARMCHAIR (Buses)

RIB8739	Leyland Atlantean AN68A/1R	Eastern Coach Works	H43/31F	1976	Ex Ribble, 1992
GIL8494	Leyland Atlantean AN68A/1R	East Lancashire	H45/31F	1978	Ex Mercer, Grimsargh, 1991
GIL8495	Leyland Atlantean AN68A/1R	East Lancashire	H45/29D	1978	Ex Mercer, Grimsargh, 1991
GIL8496	Leyland Atlantean AN68A/1R	East Lancashire	H45/29D	1978	Ex Mercer, Grimsargh, 1991
GIL2603	Leyland Atlantean AN68A/1R	Roe	H45/31F	1979	Ex South Yorkshire, 1990
GIL2604	Leyland Atlantean AN68A/1R	Roe	H45/31F	1979	Ex South Yorkshire, 1990
GIL2605	Leyland Atlantean AN68A/1R	Roe	H45/31F	1979	Ex South Yorkshire, 1990
MUH289X	Leyland Olympian ONLXB/1R	Eastern Coach Works	H45/32F	1982	Ex Rhondda, 1995
C449SJU	Ford Transit 190D	Robin Hood	B16F	1985	Ex Easton, Ramsgate, 1996
C322RPE	Ford Transit 190D	Carlyle	B16F	1986	Ex London Buslines, 1995
D829UTF	Ford Transit 190D	Carlyle	B16F	1986	Ex London Buslines, 1995
E991NMK	Leyland Swift LBM6T/2RA	Wadham Stringer Vanguard II	B37F	1988	
G94VMM	Mercedes-Benz 709D	Reeve Burgess Beaver	B25F	1989	

	Leyland Olympian ONCL10/1RZ	Alexander RL	H47/30F	1990	
G361YUR		G364YUR		G367YUR	G370YUR
G362YUR		G365YUR		G368YUR	G371YUR
G363YUR		G366YUR		G369YUR	G372YUR

H755DTM	Mercedes-Benz 811D	Reeve Burgess Beaver	B33F	1990

	Leyland Olympian ON2R50C13Z4	Leyland	H47/31F	1991	
H546GKX	H550GKX	H554GKX	H559GKX	H564GKX
H547GKX	H551GKX	H556GKX	H561GKX	
H548GKX	H552GKX	H557GKX	H562GKX	
H549GKX	H553GKX	H558GKX	H563GKX	

K663NGB	Mercedes-Benz 709D	Dormobile Routemaker	B29F	1992

	Dennis Dart SLF 9.8 metre	Plaxton Pointer	B39F*	1996	*P154–160MLE are B37F
P27MLE	P31MLE	P35MLE	P157MLE	P160MLE
P28MLE	P32MLE	P154MLE	P158MLE	
P29MLE	P34MLE	P156MLE	P159MLE	

Previous Registrations

D829UTF	C331RPE	GIL2605	YKY671T	GIL8496	UDT185S
GIL2603	YKY669T	GIL8494	UDT183S	RIB8739	SFV435P
GIL2604	YKY670T	GIL8495	UDT184S		

The coach fleet is listed in the London Coach Handbook.

CAPITAL CITYBUS

Capital Citybus Ltd, Perry Road, off Chequers Lane, Dagenham, Essex, RM9 6QD

Ensignbus gained LT route 145 (Dagenham to Redbridge Station) from 21st June 1986. This was to be the start of a major operation of tendered bus services. Frontrunner Buses (South East), a division of the privatised East Midland Motor Services, began LT route 248 (Cranham to Romford) from 24th September 1988. Many more routes were acquired by both companies until on 30th June 1989 Frontrunner's operations were purchased by Ensignbus from Stagecoach, who had taken over the East Midland group. The Ensignbus business, including the Dagenham depot, was then sold to the CNT Group of Hong Kong on 29th December 1990. A new yellow livery was introduced, featuring Chinese characters in the fleetname. As a result of gaining further LT contracts, a new depot was opened at Northumberland Park in Tottenham. The Company remained under CNT control for five years until it was bought by a management-led team on 21st December 1995. A revised fleetname started appearing on vehicles following the breaking of ties with its former owner. In late 1996, a new depot was opened in Waterden Road, Hackney.

As well as the large number of LT contract services, the Company also runs routes for Essex and Hertfordshire County Councils and commercial routes in the Thurrock area of Essex.

LT routes currently operated are 67, 97, 97A, 123, 153, 158, 165, 179, 212, 215, 236, 248, 252, 257, 296, 298, 299, 318, 365, 396, 511, 616, 645, 646, 650, 651, 670, 678, D5, D6, W6, W10, ELX and school journeys on route 307. Other routes operated are 89, 173 (Essex County Council), 330, 340 on Sundays (Hertfordshire County Council), and commercial routes 324, 348, 349, 648.

The fleet carries a livery of yellow with red relief, and is based at depots in Dagenham (Chequers Lane), Northumberland Park (Marsh Lane) and Hackney (Waterden Road).

The latest single-deckers to join the substantial Capital Citybus fleet are four Optare Excels. Entering service in November 1996, these are primarily for route 396 linking Ilford with Goodmayes. Number 701 is seen in Ilford. Mike Harris

Route 67 was put out for tender during 1996 and, as with the majority of London routes thus tendered, new vehicles were specified. Capital Citybus were successful and opted for new Volvo Olympians with Northern Counties bodywork as depicted here by their 245 in Tottenham. Mike Harris

Still a relatively rare sight in the Capital Citybus fleet is an East Lancashire body. Eight examples were bought from Southampton Citybus in 1992 and another seven from Leicester Citybus in 1996. Representing the latter examples is 344 at Upminster Station in June 1996. Mike Harris

Twenty-three single-doored Leyland bodied Leyland Olympians were bought new in 1991 by Capital Citybus for newly tendered route 123. Number 153 is one such example seen in Westbury Road near Turnpike Lane in June 1996. Gerald Mead

The only Alexander RL bodied Leyland Olympians purchased new by the company were a batch of eight bought in 1989. Seen on schooldays only route 645 in Ilford is 124 in June 1996. This particular member of the batch has recently been withdrawn. Mike Harris

Unique within the Capital Citybus fleet is this Wadham Stringer Portsdown bodied Dennis Dart purchased from Wealden Beeline in 1996. This and East Surrey's example are the only Portsdowns in the London area. No.669 is seen here at Palmers Green. Mike Harris

During 1996, additional Volvo B6s were sought to cover extra work which resulted in a trio of Northern Counties Paladins being purchased from Flightpath of Gatwick Airport. One of them is 685 seen at the vast Lakeside Shopping Centre complex in May 1996 on route 349. Mike Harris

One of the shortest routes in the London area is the Capital Citybus operated W10.
Running between Enfield Town and Crews Hill Station on Monday to Saturday shopping
hours only, the route uses a Mercedes-Benz minibus from the route 299 allocation and
612 was pictured in Enfield Town in April 1996. Laurie Rufus

Ten Optare MetroRiders were purchased by Capital Citybus in 1992 and are usually to be
found on routes 298 and 299. August 1996 finds 628 at Muswell Hill Broadway on route
299. Mike Harris

Although Capital Citybus have purchased mostly new buses during the last few years, second hand examples are still occasionally acquired. The latest examples to join the fleet are a pair of former Eastbourne Buses Volvo B10Ms with Duple Dominant bodies for use on school route 646. However, one is seen here working its usual Saturday allocation on route 348 at Lakeside Shopping Centre during November 1996. Colin Lloyd

Acquired from London Coaches, but previously evaluation buses with London Buses, a pair of Dennis Dominators with Northern Counties bodies were purchased in 1993. Seen in Western Road Romford in May 1996, 202 had yet to receive new Capital Citybus logos, instead retaining the CNT Group emblems. Mike Harris

Numerically the lowest numbered vehicle in the Capital Citybus fleet is this single-doored MCW Metrobus acquired during 1996 from MTL in Liverpool. Although some fifteen years old, the bus looked resplendent when seen in Tottenham in June 1996.
Gerald Mead

CAPITAL CITYBUS

100	JHE144W	MCW Metrobus DR104/6	MCW		H46/31F	1981	Ex MTL, Liverpool, 1996
101	JHE171W	MCW Metrobus DR104/6	MCW		H46/31F	1981	Ex South Yorkshire, 1991
102	JHE172W	MCW Metrobus DR104/6	MCW		H46/31F	1981	Ex South Yorkshire, 1991
103	JHE196W	MCW Metrobus DR104/6	MCW		H46/31F	1981	Ex South Yorkshire, 1991
104	JHE194W	MCW Metrobus DR104/6	MCW		H46/31F	1981	Ex Mainline, Sheffield, 1991
105	JHE138W	MCW Metrobus DR104/6	MCW		H46/31F	1981	Ex Stevensons,1995
106	JHE157W	MCW Metrobus DR104/6	MCW		H46/31F	1981	Ex South Yorkshire, 1991
107	G107FJW	MCW Metrobus DR102/70	MCW		H43/30F	1989	Ex Optare, Leeds, 1992
108	JHE178W	MCW Metrobus DR104/6	MCW		H45/31F	1981	Ex South Yorkshire, 1991
109	JHE152W	MCW Metrobus DR104/6	MCW		H46/31F	1981	Ex MTL, Liverpool, 1996
110	JHE170W	MCW Metrobus DR104/6	MCW		H46/31F	1981	Ex South Yorkshire, 1991
111	JHE156W	MCW Metrobus DR102/28	MCW		H46/31F	1981	Ex MTL, Liverpool, 1996
112	GRA102V	MCW Metrobus DR102/4	MCW		H43/30F	1980	Ex Derby, 1990

113–120   MCW Metrobus DR104/6   MCW   H46/31F   1981   Ex South Yorkshire, 1991

113	JHE169W	115	JHE182W	117	JHE147W	119	JHE149W
114	JHE162W	116	JHE146W	118	JHE148W	120	JHE150W

121–128   Leyland Olympian ONCL10/1RZ   Alexander RL   H47/30F   1990

121	G121YEV	123	G123YEV	126	G126YEV
122	G122YEV	125	G125YEV	128	G128YEV

129	J129YRM	Leyland Olympian ON2R50C13Z4	Northern Counties Palatine	H47/30F	1991
130	J130YRM	Leyland Olympian ON2R50C13Z4	Northern Counties Palatine	H47/30F	1991
131	J131YRM	Leyland Olympian ON2R50C13Z4	Northern Counties Palatine	H47/30F	1991
132	J132YRM	Leyland Olympian ON2R50C13Z4	Northern Counties Palatine	H47/30F	1991
133	G133ATW	Leyland Olympian ONCL10/1RZ	Northern Counties Palatine	H45/30F	1989
134	J134YRM	Leyland Olympian ON2R50C13Z4	Northern Counties Palatine	H47/30F	1991
135	J135YRM	Leyland Olympian ON2R50C13Z4	Northern Counties Palatine	H47/30F	1991

136–158   Leyland Olympian ON2R50C13Z4   Leyland   H47/29F   1991

136	J136YRM	141	J141YRM	146	J146YRM	151	J151YRM	156	J156YRM
137	J137YRM	142	J142YRM	147	J247YRM	152	J152YRM	157	J157YRM
138	J138YRM	143	J143YRM	148	J148YRM	153	J153YRM	158	J158YRM
139	J139YRM	144	J144YRM	149	J149YRM	154	J154YRM		
140	J140YRM	145	J145YRM	150	J150YRM	155	J155YRM		

159–165 Leyland Olympian ON2R50C13Z4 Northern Counties Palatine H47/30F 1992

| 159 | K888TTT | 161 | K888TWY | 163 | K888PFD | 165 | K888BWU |
| 160 | K888ELR | 162 | K888LAD | 164 | K888BFG | | |

No.	Reg	Chassis	Body	Type	Year	Notes
166	K888TKS	Leyland Olympian ON2R50C13Z4	Northern Counties Palatine II	H46/29F	1993	
167	L888YTT	Volvo Olympian YN2RV18Z4	Northern Counties Palatine II	H47/29F	1993	
168	L888TTT	Volvo Olympian YN2RV18Z4	Northern Counties Palatine II	H47/29F	1993	
169	E964PME	Leyland Olympian ONLXB/1RH	Optare	H47/29F	1988	Ex Ensign, Rainham, 1994
170	E470SON	MCW Metrobus DR102/63	MCW	H45/30F	1988	Ex London Buses, 1992
171	E461SON	MCW Metrobus DR102/63	MCW	H45/30F	1988	Ex London Buses, 1992
172	C372CAS	Leyland Olympian ONLXB/1RH	Alexander RL	H47/25F	1986	Ex Highland Scottish, 1992
173	C373CAS	Leyland Olympian ONLXB/1RH	Alexander RL	H47/25F	1986	Ex Highland Scottish, 1992
174	C374CAS	Leyland Olympian ONLXB/1RH	Alexander RL	H47/25F	1986	Ex Highland Scottish, 1992
175	DAE510W	MCW Metrobus DR103/4	MCW	CH43/30F	1980	Ex MTL, Liverpool, 1996
176	DAE512W	MCW Metrobus DR103/4	MCW	CH43/30F	1980	Ex MTL, Liverpool, 1996
177	DAE513W	MCW Metrobus DR103/4	MCW	CH43/30F	1980	Ex MTL, Liverpool, 1996
178	E478SON	MCW Metrobus DR102/63	MCW	H45/30F	1988	Ex London Buses, 1992
179	E472SON	MCW Metrobus DR102/63	MCW	H45/30F	1988	Ex London Buses, 1992
180	A183WEV	Leyland Olympian ONLXB/1R	Alexander RL	H45/34F	1984	Ex Highland Scottish, 1992
181	J181HME	Dennis Dominator DDA2004	Northern Counties Palatine	H45/29F	1991	
182	J182HME	Dennis Dominator DDA2002	Northern Counties Palatine	H45/29F	1991	
183	B443CKW	Dennis Dominator DDA901	Alexander RH	H46/32F	1984	Ex Mainline, Sheffield, 1994
184	B444CKW	Dennis Dominator DDA901	Alexander RH	H46/32F	1984	Ex Mainline, Sheffield, 1994

185–189 Dennis Dominator DDA157 Alexander RH H45/33F 1982 Ex Kelvin Central Buses, 1995

| 185 | DEM83X | 186 | CHF346X | 187 | CHF347X | 188 | CHF348X | 189 | CHF349X |

190	B440CKW	Dennis Dominator DDA901	Alexander RH	H46/32F	1984	Ex Mainline Sheffield, 1995

191–198 Dennis Dominator DDA1023 East Lancashire H45/31F 1988 Ex Southampton Citybus, 1992

| 191 | F291PTP | 193 | F293PTP | 195 | F295PTP | 197 | F297PTP |
| 192 | F292PTP | 194 | F294PTP | 196 | F296PTP | 198 | F298PTP |

No.	Reg	Chassis	Body	Type	Year	Notes
199	CHF353X	Dennis Dominator DDA157	Alexander RH	H45/33F	1982	Ex Kelvin Central Buses, 1995
200	CHF350X	Dennis Dominator DDA157	Alexander RH	H45/33F	1982	Ex Kelvin Central Buses, 1995
201	CHF351X	Dennis Dominator DDA157	Alexander RH	H45/33F	1982	Ex Kelvin Central Buses, 1995
202	B102WUW	Dennis Dominator DDA1001	Northern Counties	H43/31F	1984	Ex London Coaches, 1993
203	B103WUW	Dennis Dominator DDA1001	Northern Counties	H43/31F	1984	Ex London Coaches, 1993
204	DEM84X	Dennis Dominator DDA157	Alexander RH	H45/33F	1982	Ex Kelvin Central Buses, 1995

223–238 Volvo Olympian YV3YNA413V Alexander (Belfast) H47/25D 1997 Red livery

223	P223MPU	227	P227MPU	231	P231MPU	235	P235MPU
224	P224MPU	228	P228MPU	232	P232MPU	236	P236MPU
225	P225MPU	229	P229MPU	233	P233MPU	237	P237MPU
226	P226MPU	230	P230MPU	234	P234MPU	238	P238MPU

239–249 Volvo Olympian YN2RV18Z4 Northern Counties Palatine I H47/27D 1996

239	P239HMD	242	P242HMD	245	P245HMD	248	P248HMD
240	P240HMD	243	P243HMD	246	P246HMD	249	P249HMD
241	N241CMP	244	N244CMP	247	N247CMP		

250	J135PVC	Leyland Olympian ON2R50C13Z4	Leyland	H47/25D	1991	Ex Volvo, Warwick, 1991 Red livery

251–274 Dennis Dominator DDA2001 Northern Counties Palatine H47/29D 1990/1 *Red livery

251	H251KVX	256	H256KVX	261	H261KVX	266	H266KVX	271	H271KVX
252	H252KVX	257	H257KVX	262	H262KVX	267	H267KVX	272	H272KVX
253	H253KVX	258	H258KVX	263	H263KVX	268*	H268KVX	273	H273KVX
254	H254KVX	259	H259KVX	264	H264KVX	269	H269KVX	274*	H274KVX
255	H255KVX	260	H460KVX	265	H265KVX	270	H270KVX		

275	FUT39V	MCW Metrobus DR102/14	MCW	H45/27D	1980	Ex Leicester, 1990
276	FUT36V	MCW Metrobus DR102/14	MCW	H47/27D	1980	Ex Leicester, 1990
277	FUT37V	MCW Metrobus DR102/14	MCW	H47/27D	1980	Ex Leicester, 1990
278	FUT38V	MCW Metrobus DR102/14	MCW	H46/27D	1980	Ex Leicester, 1990

279–293

MCW Metrobus DR102/71 — MCW — H46/31F — 1988

No.	Reg.	No.	Reg.	No.	Reg.	No.	Reg.	No.	Reg.
279	F279NHJ	282	F282NHJ	285	F285NHJ	288	F288NHJ	291	F291NHJ
280	F280NHJ	283	F283NHJ	286	F286NHJ	289	F289NHJ	293	F293NHJ
281	F281NHJ	284	F284NHJ	287	F287NHJ	290	F290NHJ	294	F294NHJ

295–299

MCW Metrobus DR104/3 — MCW — H46/30F — 1980 — Ex South Yorkshire, 1988

No.	Reg.	No.	Reg.	No.	Reg.	No.	Reg.	No.	Reg.
295	JWF495W	296	JWF496W	297	JWF497W	298	JWF498W	299	JWF499W

340–348

Dennis Dominator DDA1024 — East Lancashire — H46/33F — 1989 — Ex Leicester Citybus, 1996

No.	Reg.	No.	Reg.	No.	Reg.	No.	Reg.
340	F140MBC	342	F142MBC	345	F145MBC	348	F148MBC
341	F141MBC	344	F144MBC	347	F147MBC		

401–416

Dennis Arrow — Northern Counties Palatine II — H49/35F* 1996 — *413–416 are H47/35F

No.	Reg.	No.	Reg.	No.	Reg.	No.	Reg.
401	P901HMH	405	P905HMH	409	P909HMH	413	P413MTW
402	P902HMH	406	P906HMH	410	P910HMH	414	P414MTW
403	P903HMH	407	P907HMH	411	P911HMH	415	P415MTW
404	P904HMH	408	P908HMH	412	P912HMH	416	P416MTW

429 XMD81A — AEC Routemaster R2RH — Park Royal — H36/28R — 1960 — Ex Rotherham & District, 1991

601–620

Mercedes-Benz 811D — Plaxton Beaver — B28F — 1992

No.	Reg.	No.	Reg.	No.	Reg.	No.	Reg.
601	J601HMF	610	J610HMF	613	J613HMF	617	J617HMF
602	J602HMF	611	J611HMF	615	J615HMF	618	J618HMF
605	J605HMF	612	J612HMF	616	J616HMF	620	J620HMF

621–630

Optare MetroRider — Optare — B28F — 1992

No.	Reg.	No.	Reg.	No.	Reg.	No.	Reg.	No.	Reg.
621	J621HMH	623	J623HMH	625	J625HMH	627	J627HMH	629	J629HMH
622	J622HMH	624	J624HMH	626	J626HMH	628	J628HMH	630	J630HMH

No.	Reg.	Chassis	Body	Seating	Year	Notes
631	J631HMH	Mercedes-Benz 811D	Alexander AM	B28F	1992	
632	J632HMH	Mercedes-Benz 811D	Alexander AM	B28F	1992	
633	J633HMH	Mercedes-Benz 811D	Alexander AM	B28F	1992	
669	J459JOW	Dennis Dart 9SDL3011	Wadham Stringer Portsdown	B37F	1991	Ex Wealden PSV, Five Oak Green, 1995
670	L670SMC	Dennis Dart 9SDL3034	Northern Counties Paladin	B31F	1994	

671–680

Volvo B6–41 — Alexander Dash — B31F — 1994

No.	Reg.	No.	Reg.	No.	Reg.	No.	Reg.	No.	Reg.
671	L671RMD	673	L673RMD	675	L675RMD	677	L677RMD	679	L679RMD
672	L672RMD	674	L674RMD	676	L676RMD	678	L678RMD	680	L680RMD

No.	Reg.	Chassis	Body	Seating	Year	Notes
681	L281RML	Volvo B6–50	Northern Counties Paladin	B39F	1994	
682	L888JTC	Volvo B6–50	Northern Counties Paladin	B39F	1994	
683	L888AMY	Volvo B6–50	Northern Counties Paladin	B39F	1994	
684	L4GML	Volvo B6–50	Northern Counties Paladin	B31F	1994	Ex Flightpaths, Gatwick, 1996
685	L5GML	Volvo B6–50	Northern Counties Paladin	B31F	1994	Ex Flightpaths, Gatwick, 1996
686	L6GML	Volvo B6–50	Northern Counties Paladin	B31F	1994	Ex Flightpaths, Gatwick, 1996
701	P701 HMT	Optare Excel	Optare	B41F	1997	On order
702	P702 HMT	Optare Excel	Optare	B41F	1997	On order
703	P703 HMT	Optare Excel	Optare	B41F	1997	On order
704	P704 HMT	Optare Excel	Optare	B41F	1997	On order
736	THX176S	Leyland National 10351A/2R		B44F	1978	Ex London Buses, 1993
737	YYE288T	Leyland National 10351A/2R		B44F	1979	Ex London Buses, 1993
738	KRS538V	Leyland National 2 NL106L11/1R		B44F	1980	Ex Bluebird Northern, 1993
739	KRS539V	Leyland National 2 NL106L11/1R		B44F	1980	Ex Bluebird Northern, 1993
740	KRS534V	Leyland National 2 NL106L11/1R		B44F	1980	Ex Bluebird Northern, 1993
741	KRS541V	Leyland National 2 NL106L11/1R		B44F	1980	Ex Bluebird Northern, 1993
742	MSO11W	Leyland National 2 NL106L11/1R		B44F	1980	Ex Bluebird Northern, 1993
744	GUW454W	Leyland National 2 NL106AL11/2R		B41F	1981	Ex London Buses, 1994
748	B358LOY	Leyland National 2 NL116TL11/3R		B48F	1984	Ex British Airways, 1993
749	B359LOY	Leyland National 2 NL116TL11/3R		B49F	1984	Ex British Airways, 1993
750	NLP389V	Leyland National 2 NL116L11/3R		B49F	1980	Ex British Airways, 1993
751	NLP391V	Leyland National 2 NL116L11/3R		B49F	1980	Ex British Airways, 1993
797	D497MYS	Volvo B10M–61	Duple Dominant	B55F	1986	Ex Eastbourne, 1996
799	D499MYS	Volvo B10M–61	Duple Dominant	B55F	1986	Ex Eastbourne, 1996

Previous Registrations

A183WEV	A980OST	KRS534V	GSO1V	KRS541V	GSO7V
DEM83X	ACM768X	KRS538V	GSO4V	XMD81A	WLT429
DEM84X	ACM769X	KRS539V	GSO5V		

February 1997 saw this red and yellow livery introduced by Capital Citybus for route 91. No.268 is one of two Dominators to carry it. Mike Harris

Other recent double deckers to augment the extensive Capital Citybus fleet are sixteen Dennis Arrows with Northern Counties Palatine II bodies. Included in this total were seven for newly won tendered route 179 whilst five, including 404 pictured here turning into Aldgate Bus Station in September 1996, are for route ELX, the 'temporary' East London Underground replacement bus service. Those for route 179 are in corporate fleet livery, those for the ELX carry a special dedicated orange livery. Geoff Rixon

CAPITAL COACHES

Capital Coaches Ltd, Heathrow Coach Centre, Sipson Road, West Drayton, UB7 0HN

Capital Coaches operate a large fleet of coaches on external and internal contract services at both Heathrow and Gatwick Airports, with a few Dennis Darts employed on airport car park duties.

The firm entered tendered bus work in August 1993 with the acquisition of LT route H26, initially using four Mercedes-Benz minibuses. Later in 1993, these were superseded by new wheelchair-accessible Mercedes-Benz minibuses with Plaxton Beaver bodies. In November 1996, the Company was successful in retaining the route upon re-tendering.

Fleet livery is white and yellow, and vehicles are kept at Sipson Road and at Eastern Perimeter Road, Heathrow.

CAPITAL COACHES

H837GLD	Mercedes-Benz 609D	North West Coach Sales	C13F	1991	Ex Marton, West Drayton, 1992
L204ULX	Mercedes-Benz 709D	Plaxton Beaver	B18FL	1993	
L205ULX	Mercedes-Benz 709D	Plaxton Beaver	B18FL	1993	
L206ULX	Mercedes-Benz 709D	Plaxton Beaver	B18FL	1993	

The coach fleet is listed in the London Coach Handbook.

A trio of Plaxton Beaver bodied Mercedes-Benz 709Ds was bought by Capital Coaches during 1993 to replace 1991 examples. These are used exclusively on LT route H26, still the only route operated by this company. Photographed at Hatton Cross Station in April 1995, L206ULX shows off its London Borough of Hounslow sponsorship logo. Colin Lloyd

CENTREWEST

CentreWest London Buses Ltd, Telstar House, Eastbourne Terrace, London W2 6LG

CentreWest was purchased from London Buses by a management-led team on 2nd September 1994, taking 507 vehicles. Apart from 30 full-size vehicles, all of the single-deckers were midibuses, CentreWest having made the greatest strides of the LBL subsidiaries in converting routes to this format.

In December 1995 CentreWest took over a number of LT contract routes in the Orpington area, re-opening the former Kentish Bus depot at Swanley for the purpose before occupying a new site at St Mary Cray in March 1996. In March 1996, the holding company of CentreWest also purchased the Bee Line and London Buslines companies, and some interchange of vehicles has since taken place between the fleets, particularly to improve the age profile of these acquired operations.

The fleet operates from garages at Acton Tram Depot, Alperton, Greenford, Orpington, Uxbridge and Westbourne Park. Vehicles are also allocated to the training fleet, based at various garages as required. Traditional London livery of red with white relief is still carried by the majority of the fleet, with gold fleetnames covering local marketing names which include Gold Arrow, Orpington Buses, Ealing Buses, Uxbridge Buses and Challenger.

RML2609, seen in Trafalgar Square in October 1996, shows the use of Gold Arrow fleetnames on central London work, as well as the route description which applies to common points on Routemaster routes 7 and 23. The duty number in the front of the driver's cab will also be noted. Colin Lloyd

Finding frequent use in hot summer months, and also at Christmas for the illuminations, RMC1510 is also available for private hire. Here it is seen on ordinary bus work in the Strand. Martin Ruthe

Route 207 remains one of the busier routes. This view of Metrobus M860, taken in July 1996, demonstrates the Ealing Buses fleetname used on buses provided for this service from Acton tram depot, opposite which this view was taken. Colin Brown

In the autumn of 1996, route 607 was upgraded from single-deck operation to new Volvo Olympians with Northern Counties bodywork, of which fifteen were delivered. V51, photographed in October 1996 with Uxbridge Buses fleetnames, demonstrates the livery of white panels between the decks used for this type. Geoff Rixon

Owned by London Transport, and having been demonstrated at the Coach and Bus Show at Birmingham in October 1995, DLP1, an early low-floor Dennis Dart with Plaxton bodywork, was delivered to CentreWest in the summer of 1996. It was found working on route 222, where it was used alongside the LLW class, in September 1996. Geoff Rixon

Route A10 was introduced between Uxbridge and Heathrow Airport on 31st August 1996, using seven low-floor Dennis Darts with Plaxton bodywork. L3 shows the special livery used for this operation as it pauses at Stockley Park in September 1996. Geoff Rixon

The Orpington network which was acquired at the end of 1995 entailed the use of seven Mercedes-Benz 811D vehicles with Marshall bodywork (subsequently increased to ten). MM2 loads in Bromley High Street in September 1996. Mike Harris

CENTREWEST

BL1-91
Bristol LH6L — Eastern Coach Works — B39F* — 1976-77 — * BL36 and 81 are DP40F — Ex London Buses, 1994

1t	KJD401P	34t	KJD434P	65t	OJD65R	85	OJD85R
2t	KJD402P	35t	KJD435P	69t	OJD69R	91t	OJD91R
4t	KJD404P	36t	KJD436P	78t	OJD78R		
28t	KJD428P	49t	OJD49R	81t	OJD81R		

D33-41
Dennis Dart SFD412BRSTGD1 — Plaxton Pointer — B37F — 1996

33	133CLT	35	N635ACF	37	N637ACF	39	P409MLA	41	P411MLA
34	N634ACF	36	N636ACF	38	P408MLA	40	P410MLA		

DLP1
P41MLE — Dennis Dart SFDBR1SGW1 — Plaxton Pointer — B27D — 1996 On extended loan from London Transport

DM117-157
Dennis Dart SLF — Marshall — B33F — 1997 On order

117	P117NLW	126	P126NLW	135	P135NLW	144	P144NLW	153	P153NLW
118	P118NLW	127	P127NLW	136	P136NLW	145	P145NLW	154	P154NLW
119	P119NLW	128	P128NLW	137	P137NLW	146	P146NLW	155	
120	P120NLW	129	P129NLW	138	P138NLW	147		156	P156NLW
121	P121NLW	130	P130NLW	139	P139NLW	148	P148NLW	157	P157NLW
122	P122NLW	131	P131NLW	140	P140NLW	149	P149NLW		
123	P123NLW	132	P132NLW	141	P141NLW	150	P150NLW		
124	P124NLW	133	P133NLW	142	P142NLW	151	P151NLW		
125	P125NLW	134	P134NLW	143	P143NLW	152	P152NLW		

DP1-32
Dennis Dart 9SDL3053 — Plaxton Pointer — B32F — 1995

1	N801FLW	8	N808FLW	15	N815FLW	22	N822FLW	29	N829FLW
2	N802FLW	9	N809FLW	16	N816FLW	23	N823FLW	30	N830FLW
3	N803FLW	10	N810FLW	17	N817FLW	24	N824FLW	31	N831FLW
4	N804FLW	11	N811FLW	18	N818FLW	25	N825FLW	32	N832FLW
5	N805FLW	12	N812FLW	19	N819FLW	26	N826FLW		
6	N806FLW	13	N813FLW	20	N820FLW	27	N827FLW		
7	N807FLW	14	N814FLW	21	N821FLW	28	N828FLW		

Nine standard Dennis Darts with Plaxton bodywork joined the fleet in 1996. The last four of these went to the Orpington Buses fleet, in which D38 was found at Orpington in September 1996. Martin Ruthe

DW1-14

DW1-14	Dennis Dart 8.5SDL3003	Wright Handybus	B30F	1990	Ex London Buses, 1994		

1	JDZ2301	**5**	JDZ2305	**9**	JDZ2309	**12**	JDZ2312
2	JDZ2302	**6**	JDZ2306	**10**	JDZ2310	**13**	JDZ2313
3	JDZ2303	**7**	JDZ2307	**11**	JDZ2311	**14**	JDZ2314
4	JDZ2304	**8**	JDZ2308				

DW15-126 Dennis Dart 8.5SDL3003* Wright Handybus B26F 1990-92

*DW92-9/101-14 are 8.5SDL3010, DW115-25 are 8.5SDL3015, DW126 is 8.5SDL3018   Ex London Buses, 1994

15	JDZ2315	**32**	JDZ2332	**77**	JDZ2377	**94**	JDZ2394	**111**	KDZ5111
16	JDZ2316	**33**	JDZ2333	**78**	JDZ2378	**95**	JDZ2395	**112**	KDZ5112
17	JDZ2317	**34**	JDZ2334	**79**	JDZ2379	**96**	JDZ2396	**113**	LDZ9113
18	JDZ2318	**35**	JDZ2335	**80**	JDZ2380	**97**	JDZ2397	**114**	LDZ9114
19	JDZ2319	**36**	JDZ2336	**81**	JDZ2381	**98**	JDZ2398	**115**	LDZ9115
20	JDZ2320	**37**	JDZ2337	**82**	JDZ2382	**99**	JDZ2399	**116**	LDZ9116
21	JDZ2321	**38**	JDZ2338	**83**	JDZ2383	**100**	JDZ2300	**117**	LDZ9117
22	JDZ2322	**39**	JDZ2339	**84**	JDZ2384	**101**	KDZ5101	**118**	LDZ9118
23	JDZ2323	**40**	JDZ2340	**85**	JDZ2385	**102**	KDZ5102	**119**	LDZ9119
24	JDZ2324	**41**	JDZ2341	**86**	JDZ2386	**103**	KDZ5103	**120**	LDZ9120
25	JDZ2325	**42**	JDZ2342	**87**	JDZ2387	**104**	KDZ5104	**121**	LDZ9121
26	JDZ2326	**43**	JDZ2343	**88**	JDZ2388	**105**	KDZ5105	**122**	LDZ9122
27	JDZ2327	**72**	JDZ2372	**89**	JDZ2389	**106**	KDZ5106	**123**	LDZ9123
28	JDZ2328	**73**	JDZ2373	**90**	JDZ2390	**107**	KDZ5107	**124**	LDZ9124
29	JDZ2329	**74**	JDZ2374	**91**	JDZ2391	**108**	KDZ5108	**125**	LDZ9125
30	JDZ2330	**75**	JDZ2375	**92**	JDZ2392	**109**	KDZ5109	**126**	LDZ9126
31	JDZ2331	**76**	JDZ2376	**93**	JDZ2393	**110**	KDZ5110		

DW162-170 Dennis Dart 8.5SDL3015 Wright Handybus B29F* 1993

*DW169 are B26F
Ex London Buses, 1994

162	NDZ3162	**165**	NDZ3165	**168**	NDZ3168
163	NDZ3163	**166**	NDZ3166	**169**	NDZ3169
164	NDZ3164	**167**	NDZ3167	**170**	NDZ3170

L1-7 Dennis Dart SFD212BR1TGW1 Plaxton Pointer B34F 1996

1	P401MLA	**3**	P403MLA	**5**	P405MLA	**7**	P407MLA
2	P402MLA	**4**	P404MLA	**6**	P406MLA		

L225-39 Dennis Dart SFD212BR1TGW1 Plaxton Pointer B35F 1996/7

L225-236 ex London & Country, 1996

225	N225TPK	**228**	N228TPK	**231**	N231TPK	**234**	N234TPK	**237**	P237NLW
226	N226TPK	**229**	N229TPK	**232**	N232TPK	**235**	N235TPK	**238**	P238NLW
227	N227TPK	**230**	N230TPK	**233**	N233TPK	**236**	N236TPK	**239**	P239NLW

LC1	N921LUF	LDV 400	Crystals	B12FL	1995	
LC2	N922LUF	LDV 400	Crystals	B12FL	1995	
LC3	N923LUF	LDV 400	Crystals	B12FL	1995	

LLW11-24 Dennis Lance SLF 11SDA3202 Wright Pathfinder 320 B34D 1993-94 Ex London Buses, 1994

11	ODZ8911	**14**	ODZ8914	**17**	ODZ8917	**20**	ODZ8920	**23**	ODZ8923
12	ODZ8912	**15**	ODZ8915	**18**	ODZ8918	**21**	ODZ8921	**24**	ODZ8924
13	ODZ8913	**16**	ODZ8916	**19**	ODZ8919	**22**	ODZ8922		

LN33-46 Leyland Olympian ON2R50C13Z4 Northern Counties H47/30F 1990 Ex London Buslines, 1996

33	H133FLX	**37**	H137FLX	**39**	H139FLX	**42**	H142FLX	**45**	H145FLX
36	H136FLX								

LS444-504 Leyland National 2 NL106AL11/2R (Volvo) DP43F 1981 Ex London Buses, 1994

444u	GUW444W	**472u**	GUW472W	**503u**	503CLT
470t	GUW470W	**497u**	GUW497W	**504u**	GUW504W

LX2u	292CLT	Leyland Lynx LX112L10ZR1R	Leyland	DP48F	1988	Ex London Buses, 1994
LX9	809DYE	Leyland Lynx LX112TL11ZR1R	Leyland	DP48F	1987	Ex London Buses, 1994
LX10	810DYE	Leyland Lynx LX112TL11ZR1R	Leyland	DP48F	1987	Ex London Buses, 1994
LX11	811DYE	Leyland Lynx LX112TL11ZR1R	Leyland	DP48F	1987	Ex London Buses, 1994

The last nine orthodox Dennis Darts with Wright bodywork are now with CentreWest, having started life with East London. DW165, at Golders Green in April 1996, shows the multi-coloured Harlesden Challenger fleetname used for operations on route 226 from Alperton garage. Colin Lloyd

CentreWest operate fourteen low-floor Dennis Lances with Wright bodywork on route 222. LLW23 was photographed with Uxbridge Buses fleetname at Harlington Corner in September 1996. Colin Brown

Five of the large group of Mercedes-Benz 811D vehicles with Alexander bodywork delivered for Gold Arrow services in 1988/9 have been converted for use as mobility buses. MA3 was caught in Dormers Wells Lane in June 1996. Geoff Rixon

The only members of the BL class, comprising Bristol LHs with Eastern Coach Works bodies, to survive in use with former LBL companies are those used as driver-training vehicles by CentreWest. BL81 passes along Ruislip Road, Greenford in May 1996 in the hands of a novice. Colin Lloyd

M234-583

MCW Metrobus DR101/12* MCW H43/28D 1980 *M523/83 are DR101/14
Ex London Buses, 1994 (M234/81, 385 ex London General, 1996)

234	BYX234V	337	EYE337V	368	GYE368W	414	GYE414W	487	GYE487W
281	BYX281V	338	EYE338V	369	GYE369W	418	GYE418W	489	GYE489W
285	BYX285V	339	EYE339V	370	GYE370W	421	GYE421W	494	GYE494W
291	BYX291V	340	EYE340V	371	GYE371W	425	GYE425W	497	GYE497W
305	BYX305V	343	EYE343V	374	GYE374W	427	GYE427W	498	GYE498W
308	BYX308V	345	EYE345V	383	GYE383W	434	GYE434W	499	GYE499W
311	BYX311V	347	GYE347W	385	GYE385W	442	GYE442W	504	GYE504W
316	EYE316V	349	GYE349W	390	GYE390W	451	GYE451W	505	GYE505W
319	EYE319V	358	GYE358W	393	GYE393W	452	GYE452W	523	GYE523W
329	EYE329V	360	GYE360W	397	GYE397W	465	GYE465W	583	GYE583W
330	EYE330V	362	GYE362W	406	GYE406W	470	GYE470W		
332	EYE332V	364	GYE364W	413	GYE413W	486	GYE486W		

M843-952

MCW Metrobus DR101/16 MCW H43/28D 1983 Ex London Buses, 1994

843	OJD843Y	866	OJD866Y	884	OJD884Y	898	A898SUL
851	OJD851Y	872	OJD872Y	885	OJD885Y	901	A901SUL
857	OJD857Y	874	OJD874Y	886	OJD886Y	938	A938SUL
859	OJD859Y	875	OJD875Y	887	OJD887Y	941	A941SUL
860	OJD860Y	882	OJD882Y	892	A892SUL	943	A943SUL
861	OJD861Y	883	OJD883Y	893	A893SUL	952	A952SUL

M979-1438

MCW Metrobus DR101/17* MCW H43/28D 1984-86 *M1049/51/4 are DR101/19
Ex London Buses, 1994

979	A979SYF	1245	B245WUL	1328	C328BUV	1380	C380BUV	1420	C420BUV
1049	A749THV	1246	B246WUL	1335	C335BUV	1382	C382BUV	1421	C421BUV
1051	A751THV	1247	B247WUL	1338	C338BUV	1384	C384BUV	1422	C422BUV
1054	A754THV	1256	B256WUL	1340	C340BUV	1400	C400BUV	1438	C438BUV
1144	B144WUL	1258	B258WUL	1375	C375BUV	1412	C412BUV		
1199	B199WUL	1259	B259WUL	1376	C376BUV	1415	C415BUV		
1201	B201WUL	1260	B260WUL	1377	C377BUV	1418	C418BUV		
1244	B244WUL	1267	B267WUL	1378	C378BUV	1419	C419BUV		

MA1-107

Mercedes-Benz 811D Alexander AM B28F* 1988-89 *MA1/2/10/2/34/51/5/99/100
are B26F, MA3-7 are B26FL, MA47 is B24F,
MA101-5 are DP28F
Ex London Buses, 1994

1	F601XMS	34	F634XMS	54	F954BMS	73	F673XMS	92	F692XMS
2	F602XMS	35	F635XMS	55	F955BMS	74	F674XMS	93	F693XMS
3	F603XMS	36	F636XMS	56	F656XMS	75	F675XMS	94	F694XMS
4	F604XMS	37	F637XMS	57	F657XMS	76	F676XMS	95	F695XMS
5	F605XMS	38	F638XMS	58	F658XMS	77	F677XMS	96	F696XMS
6	F606XMS	39	F639XMS	59	F659XMS	78	F678XMS	97	F697XMS
7	F607XMS	40	F640XMS	60	F660XMS	79	F679XMS	98	F698XMS
10	F610XMS	42	F642XMS	61	F661XMS	80	F680XMS	99	F699XMS
11	F611XMS	43	F643XMS	62	F662XMS	81	F681XMS	100	F700XMS
12	F612XMS	44	F644XMS	63	F663XMS	82	F682XMS	101	VLT31
13	F613XMS	45	F645XMS	64	F664XMS	83	F683XMS	102	F702XMS
18	F618XMS	46	F946BMS	65	F665XMS	84	F684XMS	103	F703XMS
22	F622XMS	47	F947BMS	66	F666XMS	85	F685XMS	104	F704XMS
23	F623XMS	48	F948BMS	67	F667XMS	86	F686XMS	105	F705XMS
26	F626XMS	49	F949BMS	68	F668XMS	87	F687XMS	106	F706XMS
27	F627XMS	50	F950BMS	69	F669XMS	88	F688XMS	107	F707XMS
28	F628XMS	51	F951BMS	70	F670XMS	89	F689XMS		
32	F632XMS	52	F952BMS	71	F671XMS	90	F690XMS		
33	F633XMS	53	F953BMS	72	F672XMS	91	F691XMS		

ML101-116

Marshall Midibus Marshall B26F 1997 On order

101	P101NLW	105	P105NLW	109	P109NLW	113	P113NLW
102	P102NLW	106	P106NLW	110	P110NLW	114	P114NLW
103	P103NLW	107	P107NLW	111		115	P115NLW
104	P104NLW	108	P108NLW	112	P112NLW	116	P116NLW

MM1-10

Mercedes-Benz 811D Marshall C16 B28F 1995/96

1	N521REW	3	N523REW	5	N525REW	7	N527REW	9	P489CEG
2	N522REW	4	N524REW	6	N526REW	8	P488CEG	10	P490CEG

MT7 G537GBD Mercedes-Benz 709D Reeve Burgess Beaver B18FL 1989 Ex London Buses, 1994

MT8	G538GBD	Mercedes-Benz 709D	Reeve Burgess Beaver	B20FL	1989	Ex London Buses, 1994
MTL5	H192RWF	Mercedes-Benz 811D	Reeve Burgess Beaver	B29F	1990	Ex London Buses, 1994
MW17	LDZ9017	Mercedes-Benz 811D	Wright	B26F	1992	Ex London Buses, 1994
RF326u	MLL963	AEC Regal IV 9821LT	Metro-Cammell	B39F	1952	Ex preservation, 1996
RH1	C501DYM	Iveco Daily 49.10	Robin Hood City Nippy	DP21F	1986	On extended loan from preservation, 1996
RMC1492u	492CLT	AEC Routemaster 6RM	Park Royal	H32/25RD	1962	Ex London Buses, 1994
RMC1510	510CLT	AEC Routemaster 6RM	Park Royal	O32/25RD	1962	Ex London Buses, 1994

RML885-2740

AEC Routemaster 7RM	Park Royal	H40/32R	1961-67	Ex London Buses, 1994

885	WLT885	**2369**	JJD369D	**2473**	JJD473D	**2542**	JJD542D	**2667**	SMK667F
2268	CUV268C	**2374**	JJD374D	**2476**	JJD476D	**2553**	JJD553D	**2672**	SMK672F
2278	CUV278C	**2378**	JJD378D	**2480**	JJD480D	**2555**	JJD555D	**2677**	SMK677F
2281	CUV281C	**2379**	JJD379D	**2486**	JJD486D	**2559**	JJD559D	**2687**	SMK687F
2291	CUV291C	**2388**	JJD388D	**2490**	JJD490D	**2602**	NML602E	**2717**	SMK717F
2309	CUV309C	**2390**	JJD390D	**2498**	JJD498D	**2609**	NML609E	**2724**	SMK724F
2313	CUV313C	**2405**	JJD405D	**2501**	JJD501D	**2623**	NML623E	**2735**	SMK735F
2352	CUV352C	**2428**	JJD428D	**2506**	JJD506D	**2647**	NML647E	**2740**	SMK740F
2357	CUV357C	**2442**	JJD442D	**2522**	JJD522D	**2656**	NML656E		
2365	JJD365D	**2467**	JJD467D	**2530**	JJD530D	**2664**	SMK664F		

RW31-90

Renault-Dodge S75	Wright	B28F	1990

31	HDZ5431	**42**	HDZ5442	**53**	HDZ5453	**64**	HDZ5464	**75**	HDZ5475
32	HDZ5432	**43**	HDZ5443	**54**	HDZ5454	**65**	HDZ5465	**76**	HDZ5476
33	HDZ5433	**44**	HDZ5444	**55**	HDZ5455	**66**	HDZ5466	**77**	HDZ5477
34	HDZ5434	**45**	HDZ5445	**56**	HDZ5456	**67**	HDZ5467	**78**	HDZ5478
35	HDZ5435	**46**	HDZ5446	**57**	HDZ5457	**68**	HDZ5468	**79**	HDZ5479
36	HDZ5436	**47**	HDZ5447	**58**	HDZ5458	**69**	HDZ5469	**80**	HDZ5480
37	HDZ5437	**48**	HDZ5448	**59**	HDZ5459	**70**	HDZ5470	**81**	HDZ5481
38	HDZ5438	**49**	HDZ5449	**60**	HDZ5460	**71**	HDZ5471	**82**	HDZ5482
39	HDZ5439	**50**	HDZ5450	**61**	HDZ5461	**72**	HDZ5472	**83**	HDZ5483
40	HDZ5440	**51**	HDZ5451	**62**	HDZ5462	**73**	HDZ5473	**84**	HDZ5484
41	HDZ5441	**52**	HDZ5452	**63**	HDZ5463	**74**	HDZ5474	**85**	HDZ5485

RW86-90

Renault-Dodge S75	Wright	DP28F	1990	Ex-London Buses, 1994

86	HDZ5486	**87**	HDZ5487	**88**	HDZ5488	**89**	HDZ5489	**90**	HDZ5490

V1-12

Volvo Olympian YN2RV18Z4	Northern Counties Palatine 2 H43/29F	1995

1	N301JBV	**4**	N304JBV	**7**	N307JBV	**10**	N310JBV
2	N302JBV	**5**	N305JBV	**8**	N308JBV	**11**	N311JBV
3	N303JBV	**6**	N306JBV	**9**	N309JBV	**12**	N312JBV

V41-55

Volvo Olympian	Northern Counties Palatine 2 DPH43/29F 1996

41	P241UCW	**45**	P245UCW	**49**	P249UCW	**53**	P253UCW
42	P242UCW	**46**	P246UCW	**50**	P250UCW	**54**	P254UCW
43	P243UCW	**47**	P247UCW	**51**	P251UCW	**55**	P255UCW
44	P244UCW	**48**	P248UCW	**52**	P252UCW		

Vehicles on loan

131	J31KLR	Mercedes-Benz 811D	Plaxton Beaver	B28F	1991	from London Buslines
132	J32KLR	Mercedes-Benz 811D	Plaxton Beaver	B28F	1991	from London Buslines
134	J34KLR	Mercedes-Benz 811D	Plaxton Beaver	B28F	1991	from London Buslines
135	J35KLR	Mercedes-Benz 811D	Plaxton Beaver	B28F	1991	from London Buslines
136	J36KLR	Mercedes-Benz 811D	Plaxton Beaver	B28F	1991	from London Buslines
DSL38	N238VPH	Dennis Dart SFD112BR1TGW1	East Lancs Spryte	B31F	1996	from London & Country
DSL51	P251APM	Dennis Dart SFD112BR1TGW1	East Lancs Spryte	B31F	1996	from London & Country
DSL52	P252APM	Dennis Dart SFD112BR1TGW1	East Lancs Spryte	B31F	1996	from London & Country

Previous registrations

VLT31	F701XMS, F903CMS	292CLT	F102GRM	809DYE	D105NDW	811DYE D111NDW
133CLT	N633ACF	503CLT	GUW503W	810DYE	D106NDW	

Named vehicles
RMC1492 *Ruby*

Special liveries
Cream: BL85.
Route 607 livery: V41-55.
Blue with route branding: L1-7.

COUNTY BUS

County Bus and Coach Co Ltd, Terminus Street, Harlow, Essex, CM20 1YD

London Country North East was privatised to the AJS Group from April 1988. County Bus and Coach Ltd was established in January 1989 as the eastern part with its head office in Harlow. The Company was sold to the Lynton Travel Group in July 1991 and re-sold in October 1994 to West Midlands. In February 1996 the Company was sold again, this time to the Cowie Group plc.

The County name is not carried on the vehicles. Instead, the trading names of Town Link, Lea Valley and Thameside are used for Harlow, Ware and Grays respectively. Since becoming part of the Cowie Group, the company has invested heavily in fleet modernisation resulting in many new vehicles, especially Dennis Darts, joining the fleet.

LT routes operated are 66, 256, 346, 444, W14, W15, W16. Other routes operated are 310, 311, 363, 370, 373, 500, 502, 505, 517 with LT agreement and other commercial routes in Essex and Hertfordshire. Most of the north-east London Mobility Bus network is also operated.

The fleet carries cream and green livery, and is based at Debden (Langston Road), Edmonton (Gibbs Road), Grays (Europa Road), Harlow (Fourth Avenue) and Ware (Marsh Lane).

Sporting the latest County Bus livery applied to their Leyland Olympian fleet is LR23 at Waltham Cross. Surprisingly, these Roe bodied vehicles are still the newest double deckers in the fleet. Keith Wood

One of a pair of MCW Metrobuses acquired from Newport in 1994, M80 is seen in Eleanor Cross Road in Waltham Cross in August 1995. Along with the Leyland Olympians, the Metrobuses are based at Ware Garage and used mainly on routes 310 and 311.
Keith Wood

The mainstay of the County Bus operations in London are Dennis Darts. DP309 is a Plaxton bodied example seen at The Cambridge in Edmonton in October 1996 while on route 444. Mike Harris

Dormobile bodied Iveco Daily MB701 in London Road, Grays with the previous Thames Side fleet name style. Keith Wood

Three new low floor Dennis Dart SLFs were introduced in late 1996 for route 395 in Hertford, although they cover the 311 service on Sundays. With bodywork by Wright Brothers of Ballymena, DWL417 is seen at the Sele Farm Estate in Hertford in October 1996. Richard Godfrey

COUNTY BUS

BOV594	HDZ8354	Bova FHD12.280	Bova Futura	C49FT	1986	Ex Smith, Birmingham, 1995
BOV595	G545JOG	Bova FHD12.290	Bova Futura	C46FT	1990	Ex Smith, Birmingham, 1995
BOV596	JIW3696	Bova FHD12.280	Bova Futura	C47FT	1988	Ex Smith, Birmingham, 1994
BTL6	BAZ7385	Leyland Tiger TRCTL11/3RH	Berkhof Everest 370	C53F	1984	Ex London Country South West, 1990

DP45	K545ORH	Dennis Dart 9SDL3016	Plaxton Pointer	B34F	1992	Ex Leaside, 1997
DP46	K546ORH	Dennis Dart 9SDL3016	Plaxton Pointer	B34F	1992	Ex Leaside, 1997
DP47	K547ORH	Dennis Dart 9SDL3016	Plaxton Pointer	B34F	1992	Ex Leaside, 1996
DP48	K548ORH	Dennis Dart 9SDL3016	Plaxton Pointer	B34F	1992	Ex Leaside, 1996

DP301-313

	Dennis Dart 9SDL3002*		Plaxton Pointer	B35F	1991	* 302-7/13 are 9SDL3011 / 309 rebodied 1992

DP301	J301WHJ	**DP304**	J304WHJ	**DP307**	J307WHJ	**DP310**	J310WHJ	**DP313**	J313WHJ
DP302	J302WHJ	**DP305**	J305WHJ	**DP308**	J308WHJ	**DP311**	J311WHJ		
DP303	J303WHJ	**DP306**	J306WHJ	**DP309**	J309WHJ	**DP312**	J312WHJ		

DP318-323

Dennis Dart 9SDL3011 — Plaxton Pointer — B35F — 1992

DP318	K318CVX	**DP320**	K320CVX	**DP322**	K322CVX
DP319	K319CVX	**DP321**	K321CVX	**DP323**	K323CVX

DP324-334

Dennis Dart SLF 9metre — Plaxton Pointer — B34F — 1996

DP324	P324HVX	**DP327**	P327HVX	**DP330**	P330HVX	**DP333**	P833HVX
DP325	P325HVX	**DP328**	P328HVX	**DP331**	P331HVX	**DP334**	P334HVX
DP326	P326HVX	**DP329**	P329HVX	**DP332**	P332HVX		

DP951	M951LYR	Dennis Dart 9.8SDL3040	Plaxton Pointer	B40F	1995	Ex Grey-Green, 1996

DPL405-414

Dennis Dart 9.8SDL3018 — Plaxton Pointer — B40F — 1993

DPL405	K405FHJ	**DPL407**	K407FHJ	**DPL409**	K409FHJ	**DPL411**	K411FHJ	**DPL413**	K413FHJ
DPL406	K406FHJ	**DPL408**	K408FHJ	**DPL410**	K410FHJ	**DPL412**	K412FHJ	**DPL414**	K414FHJ

DW314	J314XVX	Dennis Dart 9SDL3011	Wright Handybus	B35F	1992	
DW315	J315XVX	Dennis Dart 9SDL3011	Wright Handybus	B35F	1992	
DW316	J316XVX	Dennis Dart 9SDL3011	Wright Handybus	B35F	1992	
DW317	J317XVX	Dennis Dart 9SDL3011	Wright Handybus	B35F	1992	
DWL401	J401XVX	Dennis Dart 9.8SDL3012	Wright Handybus	B40F	1992	
DWL402	J402XVX	Dennis Dart 9.8SDL3012	Wright Handybus	B40F	1992	
DWL403	J403XVX	Dennis Dart 9.8SDL3012	Wright Handybus	B40F	1992	
DWL404	J404XVX	Dennis Dart 9.8SDL3012	Wright Handybus	B40F	1992	
DWL415	L415NHJ	Dennis Dart 9.8SDL3025	Wright Handybus	B40F	1994	
ELW266	M266VPU	Dennis Lance SLF11SDA3201	Wright Pathfinder 320	B40F	1994	
ELW267	M267VPU	Dennis Lance SLF11SDA3201	Wright Pathfinder 320	B40F	1994	
ELW268	M268VPU	Dennis Lance SLF11SDA3201	Wright Pathfinder 320	B40F	1994	
ELW269	M269VPU	Dennis Lance SLF11SDA3201	Wright Pathfinder 320	B40F	1994	
LD554	FYX814W	Leyland Leopard PSU3E/4R	Duple Dominant II Exp	C49F	1980	Ex Davian, Enfield, 1991
LP5	FYT335V	Leyland Leopard PSU3E/4R	Plaxton Supreme IV Exp	C49F	1979	Ex Cowie Leaside, 1996
LP6	FYT336V	Leyland Leopard PSU3E/4R	Plaxton Supreme IV Exp	C49F	1979	Ex Cowie Leaside, 1996

LR1-23

Leyland Olympian ONTL11/1R — Roe — H43/29F — 1982 — Ex London Country North East, 1989

LR1	TPD101X	**LR4**	TPD104X	**LR9**	TPD109X	**LR15**	TPD115X
LR2	TPD102X	**LR5**	TPD105X	**LR10**	TPD110X	**LR17**	TPD117X
LR3	TPD103X	**LR7**	TPD107X	**LR11**	TPD111X	**LR23**	TPD123X

LX251-258

Leyland Lynx LX2R11C15Z4S — Leyland — B49F — 1990

LX251	H251GEV	**LX253**	H253GEV	**LX255**	H255GEV	**LX257**	H257GEV
LX252	H252GEV	**LX254**	H254GEV	**LX256**	H256GEV	**LX258**	H258GEV

LX888	E888KYW	Leyland Lynx LX1126LXCTZR1	Leyland	B47F	1987	Ex Grey-Green, 1996
LX889	E889KYW	Leyland Lynx LX1126LXCTZR1	Leyland	B47F	1987	Ex Grey-Green, 1996
M75	JBO75W	MCW Metrobus DR102/20	MCW	H46/31F	1981	Ex Newport, 1994
M80	JBO80W	MCW Metrobus DR102/20	MCW	H46/31F	1981	Ex Newport, 1994
MB45	D45OKH	Iveco Daily 49.10	Robin Hood City Nippy	DP19F	1987	Ex London Country North East, 1989
MB52	E352NEG	Iveco Daily 49.10	Robin Hood City Nippy	DP19F	1988	Ex London Country North East, 1989
MB53	E353NEG	Iveco Daily 49.10	Robin Hood City Nippy	DP19F	1988	Ex London Country North East, 1989
MB54	E354NEG	Iveco Daily 49.10	Robin Hood City Nippy	DP19F	1988	Ex London Country North East, 1989

MB115	F115JGS	Iveco Daily 49.10		Robin Hood City Nippy	B25F	1988	Ex Sampsons, Hoddesdon, 1989
MB154	F154DKU	Iveco Daily 49.10		Reeve Burgess Beaver	DP25F	1988	Ex demonstrator, 1989
MB343	E343SWY	Iveco Daily 49.10		Robin Hood City Nippy	B23F	1988	Ex Keighley & District, 1993
MB706	E296VOM	Iveco Daily 49.10		Carlyle Dailybus 2	B23F	1988	Ex Southend, 1992

MB707-712 Iveco Turbo Daily 59.12 — Dormobile Routemaker — B25F — 1993

MB707	K707FNO	**MB709**	K709FNO	**MB711**	K711FNO
MB708	K708FNO	**MB710**	K710FNO	**MB712**	K712FNO

MB717-744 Iveco Turbo Daily 59.12 — Marshall C31 — B25F — 1994/5

MB717	L717OVX	**MB723**	L723PHK	**MB729**	M729UTW	**MB735**	M735AOO
MB718	L718OVX	**MB724**	L724PHK	**MB730**	M730AOO	**MB736**	M736AOO
MB719	M719UTW	**MB725**	M725UTW	**MB731**	M731AOO	**MB737**	M737AOO
MB720	M720UTW	**MB726**	M726UTW	**MB732**	M732AOO	**MB738**	M738AOO
MB721	M721UTW	**MB727**	M727UTW	**MB733**	M733AOO	**MB739**	N739AVW
MB722	L722OVX	**MB728**	M728UTW	**MB734**	M734AOO	**MB740**	N740AVW

MB741	N741AVW
MB742	N742AVW
MB743	N743AVW
MB744	N744AVW

MB748	E448TYG	Iveco Daily 49.10		Robin Hood City Nippy	DP25F	1988	Ex Keighley & District, 1993
MB751	E451TYG	Iveco Daily 49.10		Robin Hood City Nippy	B23F	1988	Ex Keighley & District, 1992
MB795	F795JKX	Iveco Daily 49.10		Reeve Burgess Beaver	B21F	1988	Ex Welwyn & Hatfield, 1992
MB796	F796JKX	Iveco Daily 49.10		Reeve Burgess Beaver	B21F	1988	Ex Welwyn & Hatfield, 1992

MB918-938 Mercedes-Benz 709D — Reeve Burgess Beaver* — B23F — 1989-92
* MB933-8 are Plaxton Beaver

MB918	G918UPP	**MB926**	G926WGS	**MB930**	G930WGS	**MB934**	J934WHJ
MB919	G919UPP	**MB927**	G927WGS	**MB931**	G931WGS	**MB935**	J935WHJ
MB924	G924WGS	**MB928**	G928WGS	**MB932**	G932WGS	**MB936**	J936WHJ
MB925	G925WGS	**MB929**	G929WGS	**MB933**	J933WHJ	**MB937**	J937WHJ

MB938	J938WHJ

MBT713	L713OVX	Iveco Turbo Daily 59.12	Marshall C31C	B18FL	1994	
MBT714	L714OVX	Iveco Turbo Daily 59.12	Marshall C31C	B18FL	1994	
MBT715	L715OVX	Iveco Turbo Daily 59.12	Marshall C31C	B18FL	1994	
MBT716	L716OVX	Iveco Turbo Daily 59.12	Marshall C31C	B18FL	1994	

MBT801-805 Peugeot-Talbot Freeway — TBP — B18FL — 1993/4

MBT801	L801KNO	**MBT802**	L802KNO	**MBT803**	L803KNO	**MBT804**	L804KNO	**MBT805**	L805OVX

MC540	D40MAG	Iveco Daily 49.10	Robin Hood City Nippy	C16F	1987	Ex West Yorkshire Road Car, 1989

MD601-612 Mercedes-Benz 811D — Reeve Burgess Beaver — B28F — 1991

MD601	J601WHJ	**MD604**	J604WHJ	**MD607**	J607WHJ	**MD610**	J610WHJ
MD602	J602WHJ	**MD605**	J605WHJ	**MD608**	J608WHJ	**MD611**	J611WHJ
MD603	J603WHJ	**MD606**	J606WHJ	**MD609**	J609WHJ	**MD612**	J612WHJ

MD613	L613LVX	Mercedes-Benz 811D	Dormobile Routemaker	B31F	1993	
MD614	L614LVX	Mercedes-Benz 811D	Dormobile Routemaker	B31F	1993	
SLF416	P416HVX	Dennis Dart SFD322BR1TGW1	Wright Crusader	B41F	1996	
SLF417	P417HVX	Dennis Dart SFD322BR1TGW1	Wright Crusader	B41F	1996	
SLF418	P418HVX	Dennis Dart SFD322BR1TGW1	Wright Crusader	B41F	1996	

SLF419-431 Dennis Dart SFD322BR1TGW1 — Plaxton Pointer — B43F — 1996

SLF419	P419HVX	**SLF422**	P422HVX	**SLF425**	P425HVX	**SLF428**	P428HVX
SLF420	P420HVX	**SLF423**	P423HVX	**SLF426**	P426HVX	**SLF429**	P429HVX
SLF421	P421HVX	**SLF424**	P424HVX	**SLF427**	P427HVX	**SLF430**	P430HVX

SLF431	P431HVX

STL10	BAZ7384	Leyland Tiger TRCTL11/3RH	Plaxton Paramount 3500 2	C49FT	1985	Ex London & Country, 1992
TDB61	F61FMC	Leyland Tiger TRBTL11/2RP	Duple 300	B55F	1988	Ex Sovereign, 1989
TDB62	F62FMC	Leyland Tiger TRBTL11/2RP	Duple 300	B55F	1988	Ex Sovereign, 1989
TDB63	F63FMC	Leyland Tiger TRBTL11/2RP	Duple 300	B55F	1988	Ex Sovereign, 1989
TDL37	530MUY	Leyland Tiger TRCTL11/3RH	Duple Caribbean	C55F	1984	Ex Premier, Cambridge, 1989

TDL53-65 Leyland Tiger TRCTL11/3RH — Duple 320 — C53F* — 1986 — TDL53-63 ex London & Country, 1993; TDL65 ex London Country North East, 1989 * TDL55/60/3 are C49F

TDL53	C253SPC	**TDL55**	C255SPC	**TDL63**	C263SPC
TDL54	C254SPC	**TDL60**	C260SPC	**TDL65**	C265SPC

TL13	TPC113X	Leyland Tiger TRCTL11/2R	Eastern Coach Works B51 C49F 1982 Ex Copping & Wall, Stevenage, 1991

Representing the latest minibuses introduced into the County Bus fleet during 1994 is this Marshall bodied Iveco 59.12. Seen in Hertford in July 1996 running from the Ware Garage in Marsh Lane, MB728 is one of the batch of twenty-eight examples allocated to Grays, Harlow and Ware Garages. Richard Godfrey

One of four specially liveried Ivecos allocated to Edmonton for its Mobility route network is MBT715. Friday Hill in Chingford finds the bus on route 966 although the type can be found on other non-Mobility routes when the need arises. Keith Wood

TL15	UJN634Y	Leyland Tiger TRCTL11/2R		Eastern Coach Works B51	C49F	1982	Ex Luton & District, 1991
TL20	UJN429Y	Leyland Tiger TRCTL11/2R		Eastern Coach Works B51	C49F	1982	Ex London Country North East, 1989
TL27	KIW8513	Leyland Tiger TRCTL11/2R		Eastern Coach Works B51	C49F	1982	Ex London Country North East, 1989
TL30	WPH130Y	Leyland Tiger TRCTL11/2R		Eastern Coach Works B51	C49F	1982	Ex Luton & District, 1991
TL31	WPH130Y	Leyland Tiger TRCTL11/2R		Eastern Coach Works B51	C53F	1982	Ex Chartercoach, Great Oakley, 1990
TL33	WPH133Y	Leyland Tiger TRCTL11/2R		Eastern Coach Works B51	C53F	1982	Ex Chartercoach, Great Oakley, 1990

TP61-75   Leyland Tiger TRCTL11/2RH   Plaxton Paramount 3200 2 Exp C49F   1985   TP61 ex Sovereign, 1991

TP61	B261KPF	TP70	OIB3520	TP71	OIB3521	TP72	OIB3522	TP75	OIB3523

TPL518	E118KFV	Leyland Tiger TRCTL11/3ARZ	Plaxton Paramount 3500 3	C51FT	1988	Ex Moore, Saffron Walden, 1993
VDL891	E891KYW	Volvo B10M-61	Duple 320	C53F	1988	Ex Grey-Green, 1996
VEL855	A855UYR	Volvo B10M-61	East Lancashire EL2000(1992) B49F		1984	Ex Grey-Green, 1996
VEL856	A856UYR	Volvo B10M-61	East Lancashire EL2000(1992) B49F		1984	Ex Grey-Green, 1996
VPB64	E564BNK	Volvo B10M-56	Plaxton Derwent II	B54F	1988	Ex Sampsons, Hoddesdon, 1989
VPB65	E565BNK	Volvo B10M-56	Plaxton Derwent II	B54F	1988	Ex Sampsons, Hoddesdon, 1989
VPL501	L501MOO	Volvo B10M-60	Plaxton Première 350	C49FT	1993	
VPL503	H903AHS	Volvo B10M-60	Plaxton Paramount 3500 3	C53F	1991	Ex Park, Hamilton, 1994

Vehicles on loan

M474	GYE474W	MCW Metrobus DR101/12	MCW	H43/28D	1980	On loan from Cowie Leaside
M782	KYV782X	MCW Metrobus DR101/14	MCW	H43/28D	1982	On loan from Cowie Leaside

Previous registrations

530MUY	A137RMJ	
BAZ7384	C210PPE	
BAZ7385	B106KPF	
EBZ6531	HSF487X	
FYT335V	JVF815V, 185CLT	
FYT336V	JVF816V, 205CLT	
HDZ8354	C904JOF, 245DOC, C566LOG	
JIW3696	E908UOH	
KIW8513	WPH127Y	
OIB3520	B270KPF	
OIB3521	B271KPF	
OIB3522	B272KPF	
OIB3523	B275KPF	
UJN429Y	WPH120Y	
UJN634Y	WPH115Y, KIW8513, OIB3510	

Special Liveries
All-over advertisement: LR2/4/5/15, TDP62, VPB64, MB54/706/95/918/32, TL13/20/7/33
LT Mobility Bus: MBT713–6
Sampson: TDL37, STL10, BP504/7, VPL530, VPL533, MC540, LD554, BOV594–6
Leaside Travel: LP5, TPL518, VDL891, VPL501/3

DPL424 is one of a batch of 10.6 metre SLF Darts, the longest currently available version of this chassis. They are allocated to Grays. Martin Ruthe

COWIE LEASIDE

Leaside Bus Co Ltd, 16 Watsons Road, London N22 4TZ

Leaside was purchased by the Cowie group on 29th September 1994, taking 523 vehicles.

Following livery experiments in the summer of 1995, traditional London red has been augmented by yellow relief in the form of a flying sash towards the rear of vehicles and across the front. Some interchange of vehicles has taken place with Cowie South London, and with County Bus.

The fleet operates from garages at Clapton, Enfield, Palmers Green, Stamford Hill, Tottenham and Wood Green.

Some vehicles in the private hire and contracts fleet have recently appeared in a maroon, white and blue livery for Leaside Travel.

The autumn of 1995 saw the arrival of thirteen DAF double-deckers with Northern Counties bodywork for the acquisition of contract route 263. DBS2 demonstrates the majestic lines of these vehicles at Barnet High Street in August 1996. Malc McDonald

Leaside has retained a pocket of five Leyland Titans for private hire work. T100, with Park Royal bodywork bedecked with Leaside Travel fleetnames, passes the Elephant & Castle gyratory system on its way to Chessington in May 1996. The wheel-hub covers are an addition to the normal equipment.
Colin Lloyd

Cowie Leaside have now started to repaint their refurbished RMLs with yellow relief. RML2492 was seen freshly-repainted at Angel in June 1996. Note the red-painted radiator grille. Richard Godfrey

During 1996 Leaside received seven Carlyle-bodied Dennis Darts from South London, where they had been displaced by larger vehicles, and used them to replace Optare StarRiders on route 192. DT63 prepares to accept custom at Edmonton Green bus station in October 1996. Colin Lloyd

DRL46 (with deficient fleet number transfers), a Dennis Dart with Plaxton bodywork, was photographed in New Barnet in April 1996 on route 184. Four members of this type remain in use, this example having been withdrawn in January 1997. Colin Brown

COWIE LEASIDE

AN110u	MPJ210L	Leyland Atlantean PDR1A/1Sp	Metro-Cammell-Weymann	O43/29D	1972	Ex County, 1996		

DBS1–13

DAF DB250RS505*   Northern Counties   H47/30F   1995   * DBS11–13 are DE02RSDB250

1	N601DWY	**4**	N604DWY	**7**	N607DWY	**10**	N610DWY	**13**	N613DWY
2	N602DWY	**5**	N605DWY	**8**	N608DWY	**11**	N611DWY		
3	N603DWY	**6**	N606DWY	**9**	N609DWY	**12**	N612DWY		

DMS681w	MLK681L	Daimler Fleetline CRL6	Park Royal	H44/24D	1973	Ex London Buses, 1994
DMS1868w	GHM868N	Daimler Fleetline CRL6	Metro-Cammell-Weymann	H44/24D	1975	Ex London Buses, 1994
DMS2291	THX291S	Leyland Fleetline FE30ALRSp	Metro-Cammell-Weymann	O44/28D	1977	Ex London Buses, 1994
DP1	N551LUA	DAF DE33WSSB3000	Plaxton Première 350	C49FT	1996	
DP2	N552LUA	DAF DE33WSSB3000	Plaxton Première 350	C49FT	1996	

DRL49–52

Dennis Dart 9SDL3016   Plaxton Pointer   B34F+16   1992   Ex London Buses, 1994

49	K549ORH	**50**	K550ORH	**51**	K551ORH	**52**	K552ORH

DT58–64

Dennis Dart 8.5SDL3003   Carlyle Dartline   B28F   1990   Ex South London, 1996

58	H458UGO	**60**	H460UGO	**62**	H462UGO	**64**	H464UGO
59	H459UGO	**61**	H461UGO	**63**	H463UGO		

DV1	185CLT	Volvo B10M–61	Duple 320	C53F	1988	Ex Cowie, London N16, 1996
DV2	205CLT	Volvo B10M–61	Duple 320	C53F	1988	Ex Cowie, London N16, 1996

L315–354

Leyland Olympian ON2R50C13Z4   Alexander RH   H43/25D   1992   Ex London Buses, 1994

315	J315BSH	**323**	J323BSH	**331**	J331BSH	**339**	J339BSH	**347**	J347BSH
316	J316BSH	**324**	J324BSH	**332**	J332BSH	**340**	J340BSH	**348**	J348BSH
317	J317BSH	**325**	J325BSH	**333**	J433BSH	**341**	J341BSH	**349**	J349BSH
318	J318BSH	**326**	J326BSH	**334**	J334BSH	**342**	J342BSH	**350**	J350BSH
319	J319BSH	**327**	J327BSH	**335**	J335BSH	**343**	J343BSH	**351**	J351BSH
320	J320BSH	**328**	J328BSH	**336**	J336BSH	**344**	J344BSH	**352**	J352BSH
321	J321BSH	**329u**	J329BSH	**337**	J337BSH	**345**	J345BSH	**353**	J353BSH
322	J322BSH	**330**	J330BSH	**338**	J338BSH	**346**	J346BSH	**354**	VLT32

LDR1–55

Dennis Dart 9.8SDL3054*   Plaxton Pointer   B40F   1995/96   *LDR40-55 are SFD412BR5TGD1

1	N671GUM	**9**	N679GUM	**17**	N687GUM	**43**	P843PWW	**51**	P851PWW
2	N672GUM	**10**	N680GUM	**18**	N688GUM	**44**	P844PWW	**52**	P852PWW
3	N673GUM	**11**	N681GUM	**19**	N689GUM	**45**	P845PWW	**53**	P853PWW
4	N674GUM	**12**	N682GUM	**20**	N690GUM	**46**	P846PWW	**54**	P854PWW
5	N675GUM	**13**	N683GUM	**21**	N691GUM	**47**	P847PWW	**55**	P855PWW
6	N676GUM	**14**	N684GUM	**40**	P840PWW	**48**	P848PWW		
7	N677GUM	**15**	N685GUM	**41**	P841PWW	**49**	P849PWW		
8	N678GUM	**16**	N686GUM	**42**	P842PWW	**50**	P850PWW		

M6	WYW6T	MCW Metrobus DR101/8	Metro-Cammell-Weymann	H43/28D	1978	Ex South London, 1996
M14t	WYW14T	MCW Metrobus DR101/8	Metro-Cammell-Weymann	H43/28D	1978	Ex South London, 1995
M51	WYW51T	MCW Metrobus DR101/8	Metro-Cammell-Weymann	H43/28D	1979	Ex South London, 1996
M170	BYX170V	MCW Metrobus DR101/9	Metro-Cammell-Weymann	H43/28D	1979	Ex South London, 1995
M175	BYX175V	MCW Metrobus DR101/9	Metro-Cammell-Weymann	H43/28D	1979	Ex South London, 1995

M266–500

MCW Metrobus DR101/12   Metro-Cammell-Weymann   H43/28D   1980   Ex London Buses, 1994

(M282, M304 ex South London 1996; M310/89/441/69/91 ex South London, 1995)

266	BYX266V	**336**	EYE336V	**422t**	GYE422W	**464**	GYE464W	**491**	GYE491W
282t	BYX282V	**353**	BYX353W	**426t**	GYE426W	**469t**	GYE469W	**493**	GYE493W
304u	BYX304V	**382t**	GYE382W	**441**	GYE441W	**474**	GYE474W	**500**	GYE500W
310	BYX310V	**389**	GYE389W	**445t**	GYE445W	**478t**	GYE478W		
317	EYE317V	**419**	GYE419W	**450t**	GYE450W	**485t**	GYE485W		

M474 is on extended loan to County Bus

In 1992, forty Leyland Olympians with Alexander bodywork joined the Leaside fleet. All are now based at Clapton garage. L348 was seen at Mile End Gate on route 253 in April 1996. Mike Harris

This interesting shot shows the last four of the type, lined up in numerical order at Hyde Park during the VE-Day celebrations in May 1995. These all carry Leaside Buses coaching livery. Keith Grimes

In a somewhat different category are vehicles which carry contract livery for locally-sponsored services. M1446, one of the five single-door Metrobuses acquired from Greater Manchester, shows the livery of Middlesex University, on whose feeder services it is normally used, at Wembley Park in April 1996. *Colin Lloyd*

Overall advertising is currently banished from vehicles on normal service, but has appeared on a number of driver-training vehicles. M14, one of the earliest Metrobuses, was seen in Chingford in October 1996, advertising the wares of a manufacturer of jeans. *Colin Lloyd*

Leaside has a substantial quantity of middle-aged Metrobuses, such as M688, located at Edgware Station after running in from Turnpike Lane in May 1996.
Tony Wilson

M507–798   MCW Metrobus DR101/14   Metro-Cammell-Weymann   H43/28D   1981–82   Ex London Buses, 1994
(M515 ex South London, 1995;
M537/9/53/8 ex South London, 1996)

507	GYE507W	587	GYE587W	647	KYV647X	708	KYV708X	752	KYV752X
508	GYE508W	590	GYE590W	648	KYV648X	709	KYV709X	753	KYV753X
509	GYE509W	591	GYE591W	649	KYV649X	710	KYV710X	754	KYV754X
510	GYE510W	593	GYE593W	650	KYV650X	711	KYV711X	756	KYV756X
515	GYE515W	596	GYE596W	651	KYV651X	712	KYV712X	757	KYV757X
518	GYE518W	600	GYE600W	652	KYV652X	713	KYV713X	758	KYV758X
519	GYE519W	602	GYE602W	653	KYV653X	714	KYV714X	761	KYV761X
522	GYE522W	603	GYE603W	657	KYV657X	715	KYV715X	762	KYV762X
525	GYE525W	604	GYE604W	658	KYV658X	716	KYV716X	765	KYV765X
528	GYE528W	605	GYE605W	659	KYV659X	717	KYV717X	766	KYV766X
529	GYE529W	609	KYO609X	660	KYV660X	718	KYV718X	767	KYV767X
530	GYE530W	610	KYO610X	661	KYV661X	719	KYV719X	768	KYV768X
531	GYE531W	611	KYO611X	663	KYV663X	720	KYV720X	770	KYV770X
533	GYE533W	612	KYO612X	664	KYV664X	721	KYV721X	771	KYV771X
534	GYE534W	613	KYO613X	665	KYV665X	723	KYV723X	772	KYV772X
535	GYE535W	614	KYO614X	666	KYV666X	726	KYV726X	773	KYV773X
536	GYE536W	615	KYO615X	669	KYV669X	727	KYV727X	774	KYV774X
537u	GYE537W	617	KYO617X	672	KYV672X	728	KYV728X	775	KYV775X
538	GYE538W	619	KYO619X	673	KYV673X	729	KYV729X	776	KYV776X
540	GYE540W	622	KYO622X	675	KYV675X	730	KYV730X	777	KYV777X
543	GYE543W	624	KYO624X	676	KYV676X	731	KYV731X	778	KYV778X
544	GYE544W	625	KYO625X	679	KYV679X	732	KYV732X	780	KYV780X
545	GYE545W	626	KYO626X	681	KYV681X	733	KYV733X	781	KYV781X
547	GYE547W	627	KYO627X	684	KYV684X	734	KYV734X	782	KYV782X
548	GYE548W	628	KYO628X	686	KYV686X	736	KYV736X	783	KYV783X
549	GYE549W	630	KYO630X	688	KYV688X	737	KYV737X	784	KYV784X
551	GYE551W	631	KYO631X	689	KYV689X	738	KYV738X	785	KYV785X
557	GYE557W	632	KYV632X	692	KYV692X	740	KYV740X	786	KYV786X
559	GYE559W	635	KYV635X	694	KYV694X	742	KYV742X	787	KYV787X
562	GYE562W	636	KYV636X	698	KYV698X	743	KYV743X	788	KYV788X
567	GYE567W	637	KYV637X	699	KYV699X	744	KYV744X	789	KYV789X
569	GYE569W	638	KYV638X	700	KYV700X	745	KYV745X	790	KYV790X
573	GYE573W	641	KYV641X	701	KYV701X	746	KYV746X	791	KYV791X
575	GYE575W	642	KYV642X	702	KYV702X	747	KYV747X	792	KYV792X
581	GYE581W	643	KYV643X	703	KYV703X	748	KYV748X	793	KYV793X
582	GYE582W	644	KYV644X	704	KYV704X	749	KYV749X	795	KYV795X
585	GYE585W	645	KYV645X	705	KYV705X	750	KYV750X	796	KYV796X
586	GYE586W	646	KYV646X	707	KYV707X	751	KYV751X	798	KYV798X

M782 is on extended loan to County Bus

M840u	OJD840Y	MCW Metrobus DR101/16	Metro-Cammell-Weymann	H43/28D	1983	Ex South London, 1996
M891	OJD891Y	MCW Metrobus DR101/16	Metro-Cammell-Weymann	H43/28D	1983	Ex London Buses, 1994
M903	A903SUL	MCW Metrobus DR101/16	Metro-Cammell-Weymann	H43/28D	1983	Ex London Buses, 1994
M919	A919SUL	MCW Metrobus DR101/16	Metro-Cammell-Weymann	H43/28D	1983	Ex London Buses, 1994
M929	A929SUL	MCW Metrobus DR101/16	Metro-Cammell-Weymann	H43/28D	1983	Ex London Buses, 1994
M936	A936SUL	MCW Metrobus DR101/16	Metro-Cammell-Weymann	H43/28D	1983	Ex South London, 1996
M939	A939SUL	MCW Metrobus DR101/16	Metro-Cammell-Weymann	H43/28D	1983	Ex London Buses, 1994

The concept of exclusive rear-end advertising has developed in London during recent years. M1362, based at Wood Green, is sponsored by a local enterprise training body in this view at Trafalgar Square during October 1996, taking layover before returning northbound on route 29. Colin Lloyd

M988–1437

		MCW Metrobus DR101/17*		Metro-Cammell-Weymann		H43/28D		1984–86	* M1044 is DR101/19; M1367/79 are CH43/28D; M1437 is CH43/24F Ex London Buses, 1994

988	A988SYF	1136	B136WUL	1219	B219WUL	1285	B285WUL	1318	C318BUV
996	A996SYF	1137	B137WUL	1221	B221WUL	1286	B286WUL	1319	C319BUV
998	A998SYF	1138	B138WUL	1227	B227WUL	1288	B288WUL	1320	C320BUV
1000	A700THV	1139	B139WUL	1228	B228WUL	1289	B289WUL	1321	C321BUV
1044	A744THV	1140	B140WUL	1229	B229WUL	1290	B290WUL	1322	C322BUV
1070	B70WUL	1152	B152WUL	1231	B231WUL	1291	B291WUL	1323	C323BUV
1074	B74WUL	1154	B154WUL	1233	B233WUL	1293	B293WUL	1324	C324BUV
1075	B75WUL	1155	B155WUL	1239	B239WUL	1294	B294WUL	1326	C326BUV
1109	B109WUL	1162	B162WUL	1248u	B248WUL	1295	B295WUL	1327	C327BUV
1112	B112WUL	1164	B164WUL	1249	B249WUL	1296	B296WUL	1332	C332BUV
1121	B121WUL	1165	B165WUL	1252	B252WUL	1297	B297WUL	1362	C362BUV
1122	B122WUL	1169	B169WUL	1253	B253WUL	1298	B298WUL	1367	C367BUV
1123	B123WUL	1170	B170WUL	1254	B254WUL	1299	B299WUL	1379	VLT88
1124	B124WUL	1173	B173WUL	1255	B255WUL	1300	B300WUL	1398	C398BUV
1126	B126WUL	1175	B175WUL	1263	B263WUL	1303	B303WUL	1399	C399BUV
1127	B127WUL	1176	B176WUL	1265	B265WUL	1307	C307BUV	1401	C401BUV
1128	B128WUL	1179	B179WUL	1275	B275WUL	1308	C308BUV	1402	C402BUV
1129	B129WUL	1182	B182WUL	1276	B276WUL	1309	C309BUV	1404	C404BUV
1130	B130WUL	1209	B209WUL	1278	B278WUL	1310	C310BUV	1405	C405BUV
1131	B131WUL	1210	B210WUL	1279	B279WUL	1312	C312BUV	1406	C406BUV
1132	B132WUL	1213	B213WUL	1280	B280WUL	1313	C313BUV	1413	C413BUV
1133	B133WUL	1214	B214WUL	1281	B281WUL	1314	C314BUV	1417	C417BUV
1134	B134WUL	1216	B216WUL	1282	B282WUL	1316	C316BUV	1424	C424BUV
1135	B135WUL	1217	B217WUL	1283	B283WUL	1317	C317BUV	1437	VLT12

M1443	GBU1V	MCW Metrobus DR101/6	Metro-Cammell-Weymann	H43/30F	1979 Ex London Buses, 1994	
M1444	GBU4V	MCW Metrobus DR101/6	Metro-Cammell-Weymann	H43/30F	1979 Ex London Buses, 1994	
M1445	GBU5V	MCW Metrobus DR101/6	Metro-Cammell-Weymann	H43/30F	1979 Ex London Buses, 1994	
M1446	GBU8V	MCW Metrobus DR101/6	Metro-Cammell-Weymann	H43/30F	1979 Ex London Buses, 1994	
M1447	GBU9V	MCW Metrobus DR101/6	Metro-Cammell-Weymann	H43/30F	1979 Ex London Buses, 1994	
MR102	F102YVP	MCW MetroRider MF150/115	Metro-Cammell-Weymann	B23F	1988 Ex London Buses, 1994	
MR104	F104YVP	MCW MetroRider MF150/116	Metro-Cammell-Weymann	DP23F	1988 Ex London Buses, 1994	
MR105	F105YVP	MCW MetroRider MF150/116	Metro-Cammell-Weymann	DP23F	1988 Ex London Buses, 1994	
RM5	VLT5	AEC Routemaster 5RM	Park Royal	H36/28R	1959 Ex London Buses, 1994	
RM311u	KGJ142A	AEC Routemaster 5RM	Park Royal	H36/28R	1960 Iveco engine; ex South London, 1996	
RM1125u	KGH858A	AEC Routemaster 5RM	Park Royal	H36/28R	1962 Iveco engine; ex South London, 1996	
RM1725u	725DYE	AEC Routemaster 5RM	Park Royal	H36/28R	1963 Iveco engine; ex South London, 1996	
RM2185u	CUV185C	AEC Routemaster 5RM	Park Royal	H36/28R	1965 Iveco engine; ex South London, 1996	
RMC1453	453CLT	AEC Routemaster 6RM	Park Royal	H32/25RD	1962 Ex London Buses, 1994	
RMC1464	464CLT	AEC Routemaster 6RM	Park Royal	O36/25RD	1962 Iveco engine; ex South London, 1995	

Leaside hold fourteen of the Wright-bodied low-floor Scanias which form the SLW class, using them on route 144. SLW12, photographed in Edmonton in October 1996, shows how the original livery has been modified with yellow relief to conform more closely to Cowie group standards. Colin Lloyd

RML882–2758 AEC Routemaster 7RM   Park Royal   H40/32R   1961–68   Ex London Buses, 1994: Cummins engines

882	WLT882	2330	CUV330C	2409	JJD409D	2552	JJD552D	2675	SMK675F
884	WLT884	2334	CUV334C	2416	JJD416D	2562	JJD562D	2678	SMK678F
888	WLT888	2340	CUV340C	2418	JJD418D	2567	JJD567D	2682	SMK682F
896	WLT896	2344	CUV344C	2434	JJD434D	2571	JJD571D	2684	SMK684F
897	WLT897	2346	CUV346C	2457	JJD457D	2588	JJD588D	2685	SMK685F
901	WLT901	2350	CUV350C	2460	JJD460D	2589	JJD589D	2688	SMK688F
2261	CUV261C	2354	CUV354C	2468	JJD468D	2595	JJD595D	2708	SMK708F
2267	CUV267C	2355	CUV355C	2483	JJD483D	2597	JJD597D	2716	SMK716F
2277	CUV277C	2356	CUV356C	2492	JJD492D	2611	NML611E	2742	SMK742F
2280	CUV280C	2359	CUV359C	2494	JJD494D	2617	NML617E	2746	SMK746F
2287	CUV287C	2370	JJD370D	2503	JJD503D	2625	NML625E	2747	SMK747F
2292	CUV292C	2372	JJD372D	2504	JJD504D	2628	NML628E	2750	SMK750F
2294	CUV294C	2373	JJD373D	2510	JJD510D	2632	NML632E	2754	SMK754F
2304	CUV304C	2380	JJD380D	2518	JJD518D	2635	NML635E	2758	SMK758F
2315	CUV315C	2386	JJD386D	2525	JJD525D	2638	NML638E		
2323	CUV323C	2391	JJD391D	2526	JJD526D	2643	NML643E		
2325	CUV325C	2394	JJD394D	2528	JJD528D	2655	NML655E		
2326	CUV326C	2401	JJD401D	2534	JJD534D	2658	SMK658F		
2328	CUV328C	2406	JJD406D	2544	JJD544D	2660	SMK660F		
2329	CUV329C	2408	JJD408D	2546	JJD546D	2666	SMK666F		

RV1	GJG750D	AEC Regent V 2D3RA		Park Royal	H40/32F	1966	Ex London Buses, 1994

SLW1–14   Scania N113CRL   Wright Pathfinder 320   B37D   1994   Ex London Buses, 1994

1	RDZ1701	5	RDZ1705	9	RDZ1709	13	RDZ1713
2	RDZ1702	6	RDZ1706	10	RDZ1710	14	RDZ1714
3	RDZ1703	7	RDZ1707	11	RDZ1711		
4	RDZ1704	8	RDZ1708	12	RDZ1712		

Leaside retain three MCW Metroriders for use on a shuttle contract for the DHSS. The application of new livery is shown in this view of MR102. Stephen Madden

T69	70CLT	Leyland Titan TNLXB2RRSp	Park Royal	O44/26D	1979	Ex London Buses, 1994
T83	CUL83V	Leyland Titan TNLXB2RRSp	Park Royal	H44/26D	1979	Ex London Buses, 1994
T85	CUL85V	Leyland Titan TNLXB2RRSp	Park Royal	H44/26D	1979	Ex London Buses, 1994
T95	CUL95V	Leyland Titan TNLXB2RRSp	Park Royal	H44/26D	1979	Ex London Buses, 1994
T100	CUL100V	Leyland Titan TNLXB2RRSp	Park Royal	H44/26D	1979	Ex London Buses, 1994
TPL1	124CLT	Leyland Tiger TRCTL11/3ARZM	Plaxton Paramount 3200 3	C53F	1989	Ex London Buses, 1994
TPL2	361CLT	Leyland Tiger TRCTL11/3ARZM	Plaxton Paramount 3200 3	C53F	1989	Ex London Buses, 1994
TPL8	H643GRO	Leyland Tiger TRCL10/3ARZA	Plaxton Paramount 3200 3	C53F	1991	Ex London Buses, 1994

Previous registrations

KGH858A	125CLT
KGJ142A	WLT311
VLT12	C437BUV
VLT32	J354BSH
VLT88	C379BUV
70CLT	CUL69V
124CLT	G661WMD
185CLT	E892KYW
205CLT	E893KYW
361CLT	G662WMD

Named vehicles
M1367 Senator, M1398 Ambassador, RV1 Harvey

Special liveries
Middlesex University : M336, M1443–7
Overall advertisements : M14, M282, M382, M422/45/50
North London College: M317
Leaside Travel: DP1/2, M170/5, 537/73, 625, 649, 1248, 1367/79/98 and all coaches

COWIE SOUTH LONDON

South London Transport Ltd, Brighton Road, South Croydon, Surrey, CR2 6EL

South London was purchased by the Cowie group on 10th January 1995, taking 447 vehicles. These included the largest contingent of Olympians (161) to be taken by any of the subsidiaries. Some interchange of vehicles has since taken place with Cowie Leaside.

From the autumn of 1995, traditional red livery with white relief has been augmented by a yellow flying sash towards the rear of the vehicle, carried over the roof.

The fleet operates from garages at Brixton, Croydon, Norwood and Thornton Heath.

South London has a large number of the ECW-bodied Leyland Olympians which were delivered in the mid-1980s. L8, carrying a registration which was previously used on a Routemaster, was photographed in Buckingham Palace Road in September 1996 on route 2, the last cross-centre route to have been converted to one-man operation. Colin Lloyd

Metrobuses share with Olympians the bulk of Cowie South London's double-deck work. M973 is seen at West Croydon. Martin Ruthe

COWIE SOUTH LONDON

DR20–31   Dennis Dart 8.5SDL3003   Plaxton Pointer   B28F   1991   Ex London Buses, 1994

20	H120THE	23	H123THE	26	H126THE	29	H129THE
21	H621TKU	24	H124THE	27	H127THE	30	H130THE
22	H122THE	25	H125THE	28	H128THE	31	H131THE

DRL38–44   Dennis Dart 9SDL3016   Plaxton Pointer   B34F   1992   Ex Leaside, 1996

| 38 | K538ORH | 40 | K540ORH | 42 | K542ORH | 44 | K544ORH |
| 39 | K539ORH | 41 | K541ORH | 43 | K543ORH | | |

DRL147–158   Dennis Dart 9SDL3024   Plaxton Pointer   B34F   1993   Ex London Buses, 1994

147	L247WAG	150	L150WAG	153	L153WAG	156	L156WAG
148	L148WAG	151	L151WAG	154	L154WAG	157	L157WAG
149	L149WAG	152	L152WAG	155	L155WAG	158	L158WAG

DRL201–212   Dennis Dart 9SDL3053   Plaxton Pointer   B34F   1995

201	N701GUM	204	N704GUM	207	N707GUM	210	N710GUM
202	N702GUM	205	N705GUM	208	N708GUM	211	N711GUM
203	N703GUM	206	N706GUM	209	N709GUM	212	N712GUM

DRL213–218   Dennis Dart SFD212BR5TGD1   Plaxton Pointer   B34F   1996

| 213 | P913PWW | 215 | P915PWW | 217 | P917PWW |
| 214 | P914PWW | 216 | P916PWW | 218 | P918PWW |

One of several original Routemasters to have lost its original registration elsewhere, RM1361 demonstrates the smart livery introduced for route 159 when this became an LT-contract operation. Since this shot was taken in Haymarket in August 1996, the route diagrams on the type have generally been obscured by advertising frames and the livery is being discontinued. Geoff Rixon

One of the evaluatory Leyland Olympians with ECW bodywork purchased in 1984, L1 now carries South London private hire livery. Nonetheless it still escapes regularly onto ordinary service, as depicted in Croydon in April 1996. Herbee Thomas

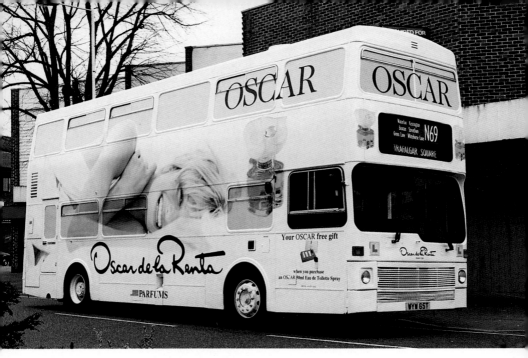

As in Leaside, South London have taken the opportunity to accept overall advertising on driver-training vehicles. M65, urging the wares of a perfume company, was seen in April 1996 blinded up for work on a night bus service. *Colin Lloyd*

At the end of 1995 South London received twelve Dennis Darts with Plaxton bodywork for the upgrading of route 412. The last of the batch, DRL212 passes through East Croydon in April 1996 on its way to Purley. *Colin Lloyd*

DT65–70 — Dennis Dart 8.5SDL3003 — Carlyle Dartline — B28F — 1990 — Ex London Buses, 1994

65	H465UGO	67	H467UGO	69	H469UGO
66	H466UGO	68	H468UGO	70	H470UGO

L1	A101SYE	Leyland Olympian ONTL11/1R	Eastern Coach Works	H47/28D	1984 Ex London Buses, 1994
L2	A102SYE	Leyland Olympian ONLXB/1R	Eastern Coach Works	H47/28D	1984 Ex London Buses, 1994
L3	A103SYE	Leyland Olympian ONLXB/1R	Eastern Coach Works	H47/28D	1984 Ex London Buses, 1994

L4–259 — Leyland Olympian ONLXB/1RH — Eastern Coach Works — H42/26D* — 1986–87

* L166–71 are DPH42/26D
Ex London Buses, 1994

No.	Reg	No.	Reg	No.	Reg	No.	Reg	No.	Reg
4	C804BYY	63	C63CHM	166	D166FYM	198	D198FYM	230	D230FYM
5	C805BYY	65	C65CHM	167	D167FYM	199	D199FYM	231	D231FYM
6	C806BYY	66	C66CHM	168	D168FYM	200	D200FYM	232	D232FYM
8	WLT807	78	C78CHM	169	D169FYM	201	D201FYM	233	D233FYM
13	VLT13	79	C79CHM	170	7CLT	202	D202FYM	234	D234FYM
14	C814BYY	99	C99CHM	171	D171FYM	203	D203FYM	235	D235FYM
16	WLT916	102	C102CHM	172	WLT372	204	D204FYM	236	D236FYM
17	C817BYY	113	C113CHM	173	VLT173	205	D205FYM	237	D237FYM
20	C820BYY	135	D135FYM	174	D174FYM	206	D206FYM	238	D238FYM
21	C21CHM	139	D139FYM	175	D175FYM	207	D207FYM	239	D239FYM
22	C22CHM	140	D140FYM	176	D176FYM	208	D208FYM	240	D240FYM
24	C24CHM	143	D143FYM	177	D177FYM	209	D209FYM	241	D241FYM
25	C25CHM	146	D146FYM	178	D178FYM	210	D210FYM	242	D242FYM
26	C26CHM	147	D147FYM	179	D179FYM	211	D211FYM	243	D243FYM
27	VLT27	148	D148FYM	180	480CLT	212	D212FYM	244	VLT244
31	C31CHM	149	D149FYM	181	D181FYM	213	D213FYM	245	D245FYM
32	C32CHM	150	D150FYM	182	D182FYM	214	D214FYM	246	D246FYM
33	330CLT	151	WLT751	183	D183FYM	215	815DYE	247	D247FYM
35	C35CHM	152	D152FYM	184	D184FYM	216	D216FYM	248	D248FYM
36	C36CHM	153	D153FYM	185	D185FYM	217	217CLT	249	D249FYM
37	C37CHM	154	WLT554	186	D186FYM	218	D218FYM	250	D250FYM
38	C38CHM	155	D155FYM	187	D187FYM	219	519CLT	251	D251FYM
41	C41CHM	156	656DYE	188	D188FYM	220	D220FYM	252	D252FYM
45	C45CHM	157	D157FYM	189	D189FYM	221	D221FYM	253	D253FYM
46	C46CHM	158	D158FYM	190	319CLT	222	D222FYM	254	D254FYM
47	VLT47	159	D159FYM	191	D191FYM	223	D223FYM	255	D255FYM
49	C49CHM	160	D160FYM	192	D192FYM	224	D224FYM	256	D256FYM
50	C50CHM	161	D161FYM	193	D193FYM	225	D225FYM	257	D257FYM
52	C52CHM	162	D162FYM	194	D194FYM	226	D226FYM	258	D258FYM
56	C56CHM	163	D163FYM	195	D195FYM	227	D227FYM	259	D259FYM
58	C58CHM	164	D164FYM	196	D196FYM	228	D228FYM		
59	C59CHM	165	D165FYM	197	D197FYM	229	D229FYM		

LDR22–39 — Dennis Dart SFD412BR5TGD1 — Plaxton Pointer — B40F — 1996

22	P822RWU	26	P826RWU	30	P830RWU	34	P834RWU	38	P838RWU
23	P823RWU	27	P827RWU	31	P831RWU	35	P835RWU	39	P839RWU
24	P824RWU	28	P828RWU	32	P832RWU	36	P836RWU		
25	P825RWU	29	P829RWU	33	P833RWU	37	P837RWU		

M7–49 — MCW Metrobus DR101/8 — Metro-Cammell-Weymann — H43/28D — 1978–79 — Ex London Buses, 1994

7t	WYW7T	10t	WYW10T	38t	WYW38T	40t	WYW40T	49t	WYW49T

M60–205 — MCW Metrobus DR101/9 — Metro-Cammell-Weymann — H43/28D — 1979 — Ex London Buses, 1994

60t	WYW60T	65t	WYW65T	74	WYW74T	149t	BYX149V	182	BYX182V
63t	WYW63T	66t	WYW66T	129	BYX129V	168	BYX168V	200	BYX200V
64	WYW64T	69	WYW69T	132t	BYX132V	173	BYX173V	205	BYX205V

M208–503 — MCW Metrobus DR101/12 — Metro-Cammell-Weymann — H43/28D — 1980 — Ex London Buses, 1994

No.	Reg	No.	Reg	No.	Reg	No.	Reg	No.	Reg
208	BYX208V	251	BYX251V	301	BYX301V	396	GYE396W	456	GYE456W
210	BYX210V	263	BYX263V	314	BYX314V	398	398CLT	458	GYE458W
220	BYX220V	277	BYX277V	346	GYE346W	399	GYE399W	492	GYE492W
225	BYX225V	280	BYX280V	365	GYE365W	400	GYE400W	496	GYE496W
230	BYX230V	283	BYX283V	372	GYE372W	402	GYE402W	503	GYE503W
232	BYX232V	290	BYX290V	378	GYE378W	410	GYE410W		
233	BYX233V	296	BYX296V	384	GYE384W	417	GYE417W		
240	BYX240V	298	BYX298V	388	GYE388W	439	GYE439W		
248	BYX248V	299	BYX299V	395	GYE395W	454	GYE454W		

M511–805 MCW Metrobus DR101/14 Metro-Cammell-Weymann H43/28D 1981–82 Ex London Buses, 1994

511	GYE511W	555	GYE555W	629	KYO629X	682	KYV682X	803	KYV803X
517	GYE517W	568	GYE568W	633	KYV633X	691	KYV691X	805	KYV805X
520	GYE520W	577	GYE577W	634	KYV634X	722	KYV722X		
521	GYE521W	580	GYE580W	654	KYV654X	724	KYV724X		
541	GYE541W	584	GYE584W	671	KYV671X	741	KYV741X		
552	GYE552W	601	GYE601W	680	KYV680X	799	KYV799X		

M809–954 MCW Metrobus DR101/16 Metro-Cammell-Weymann H43/28D 1983 Ex London Buses, 1994

809	OJD809Y	850	OJD850Y	865	OJD865Y	895	A895SUL	948	A948SUL
825	OJD825Y	858	OJD858Y	869	OJD869Y	927	A927SUL	954	WLT954
827	OJD827Y	863	OJD863Y	894	A894SUL	930	A930SUL		

M959	A959SYF	MCW Metrobus DR101/17	Metro-Cammell-Weymann	H43/28D	1984 Ex London Buses, 1994
M973	A973SYF	MCW Metrobus DR101/17	Metro-Cammell-Weymann	H43/28D	1984 Ex London Buses, 1994
M984	A984SYF	MCW Metrobus DR101/17	Metro-Cammell-Weymann	H43/28D	1984 Ex London Buses, 1994
M1036	A736THV	MCW Metrobus DR101/17	Metro-Cammell-Weymann	H43/28D	1984 Ex London Buses, 1994
M1062	B62WUL	MCW Metrobus DR101/17	Metro-Cammell-Weymann	H43/28D	1984 Ex London Buses, 1994

M1084–1105 MCW Metrobus DR134/1 Metro-Cammell-Weymann H43/28D 1984 Ex London Buses, 1994

1084	B84WUL	1089	B89WUL	1094	B94WUL	1099	B99WUL	1104	B104WUL
1085	B85WUL	1090	B90WUL	1095	B95WUL	1100	B100WUL	1105	B105WUL
1086	B86WUL	1091	B91WUL	1096	B96WUL	1101	B101WUL		
1087	B87WUL	1092	B92WUL	1097	B97WUL	1102	B102WUL		
1088	B88WUL	1093	B93WUL	1098	B98WUL	1103	B103WUL		

M1116	B116WUL	MCW Metrobus DR101/17	Metro-Cammell-Weymann	H43/28D	1984 Ex London Buses, 1994
M1354	C354BUV	MCW Metrobus DR101/17	Metro-Cammell-Weymann	H43/28D	1985 Ex London Buses, 1994
M1359	C359BUV	MCW Metrobus DR101/17	Metro-Cammell-Weymann	DPH43/28D	1985 Ex London Buses, 1994
M1407	C407BUV	MCW Metrobus DR101/17	Metro-Cammell-Weymann	H43/28D	1985 Ex London Buses, 1994
M1441	A441UUV	MCW Metrobus DR102/45	Metro-Cammell-Weymann	H43/28D	1984 Ex London Buses, 1994
M1442	A442UUV	MCW Metrobus DR132/5	Metro-Cammell-Weymann	H43/28D	1984 Ex London Buses, 1994
MR93	E873NJD	MCW MetroRider MF150/96	Metro-Cammell-Weymann	B25F	1988 Ex East London, 1995

MRL107–133 MCW MetroRider MF158/16* Metro-Cammell-Weymann B28F* 1988 *MRL133 is MF158/17 and DP28F
Ex London Buses, 1994

107	F107YVP	123	F123YVP	127	F127YVP	133	F133YVP
122	F122YVP	124	F124YVP	129	F129YVP		

RM6–2217 AEC Routemaster 5RM Park Royal H36/28R 1959–65 Iveco engines
Ex London Buses, 1994

6	VLT6	467	XVS851	997	WLT997	1593	593CLT	1978	ALD978B
18	VLT18	531	WLT531	1003	3CLT	1734	734DYE	2179	CUV179C
25	VLT25	664	WLT664	1124	VYJ806	1801	801DYE	2217	CUV217C
275	VLT275	676	WLT676	1324	324CLT	1811	EGF220B		
348	WLT348	719	WLT719	1361	VYJ808	1822	822DYE		
432	SVS617	970	WLT970	1398	KGJ118A	1872	ALD872B		

RML892–2759 AEC Routemaster 7RM Park Royal H40/32R 1961–68 Iveco engines
Ex London Buses, 1994

892	WLT892	2351	CUV351C	2521	JJD521D	2636	NML636E	2741	SMK741F
895	WLT895	2366	JJD366D	2545	JJD545D	2653	NML653E	2753	SMK753F
2264	CUV264C	2375	JJD375D	2549	JJD549D	2692	SMK692F	2759	SMK759F
2307	CUV307C	2407	JJD407D	2572	JJD572D	2718	SMK718F		
2324	CUV324C	2477	JJD477D	2573	JJD573D	2726	SMK726F		
2333	CUV333C	2491	JJD491D	2608	NML608E	2730	SMK730F		

Previous registrations

EGF220B	811DYE	VLT173	D173FYM	WLT751	D151FYM	217CLT	D217FYM	480CLT	D180FYM
KGJ118A	398CLT	VLT244	D244FYM	WLT807	C807BYY	319CLT	D190FYM	519CLT	D219FYM
SVS617	WLT432	VYJ806	124CLT	WLT916	C816BYY	324CLT	324CLT,	656DYE	D156FYM
VLT13	C813BYY	VYJ808	361CLT	WLT954	A954SUL		VYJ807	815DYE	D215FYM
VLT27	C27CHM	WLT372	D172FYM	XVS851	WLT467	330CLT	C30CHM		
VLT47	C47CHM	WLT554	D154FYM	7CLT	D170FYM	398CLT	GYE398W		

Special liveries
Overall advertisements : M65, M149

CRYSTALS

C J Springham, 127 Dartford Road, Dartford, Kent, DA1 3EN

Starting life as a taxi firm in 1970, Crystals bought their first minibus in 1972. The company was one of the first operators of LT-tendered routes when route 146 was taken over in August 1985. Although the contract was retained in 1988, it was not renewed in 1993. The Company has since been successful in obtaining many Mobility Bus routes in both south-east London and west London, the latter operating from a new base in Chelsea.

From 2nd December 1995, the Company won tendered routes R2 and R7 in the Orpington area, for which new Plaxton bodied Mercedes-Benz minibuses were purchased.

LT routes operated are R2, R7 and Mobility Bus routes 851-858, 861-870, 931-937, 970-973. Vehicles on the bus routes carry a new livery of turquoise, whilst those on Mobility Bus routes are in red with yellow relief. Vehicles are kept at Dartford (Dartford Road) and Chelsea (Hortensia Road).

CRYSTALS

F467MUF	Iveco Daily 40–8	Dormobile Routemaker	DP20F	1989	Ex Hailstone, Basildon, 1995
L68DPE	Mercedes-Benz 709D	Crystals	DP18FL	1994	
L76DPE	Mercedes-Benz 709D	Crystals	DP18FL	1994	
L168EKR	Mercedes-Benz 711D	Crystals	B18FL	1994	
M569TJL	Mercedes-Benz 709D	Crystals	B19FL	1995	
N601JGP	Mercedes-Benz 709D	Crystals	B25F	1995	
N602JGP	Mercedes-Benz 709D	Crystals	B25F	1995	
N603JGP	Mercedes-Benz 709D	Crystals	B25F	1995	
N604JGP	Mercedes-Benz 811D	Crystals	B29F	1995	
N605JGP	Mercedes-Benz 811D	Crystals	B29F	1995	
N606JGP	Mercedes-Benz 811D	Crystals	B29F	1995	
N607JGP	Mercedes-Benz 811D	Crystals	B29F	1995	

Above right **Crystals have secured the majority of the Mobility routes in south east London and Mercedes-Benz minibuses are employed. L68DPE represents a typical example in Bromley High Street whilst working route 851.** Russell Upcraft

Right **Seven new Mercedes-Benz minibuses were bought in 1995 following the gaining of routes R2 and R7 in Orpington. Four were 811D models with twenty-nine seats; three were twenty-five seaters on 709D chassis. N605JGP is seen turning into Orpington High Street during February 1996.** Colin Lloyd

DOCKLANDS MINIBUS

Docklands Transit Ltd, Magnet Shipping Warehouse, Thames Road, Silvertown, London, E16 2EE

Docklands Transit, part of the Transit Holdings Group, introduced several commercial services in the London Docklands area from March 1989 using a fleet of Mellor-bodied Ford Transits. The operation was unsuccessful and ceased in November 1990, although a few vehicles continued on contract work. However, success came during 1995 when three LT tendered routes were won in the Barking area. A fleet of Mercedes-Benz minibuses was drafted in from fellow group member Red Admiral of Portsmouth. LT tendered route 106, linking Finsbury Park with Whitechapel Station, was gained in April 1996 and eighteen new Plaxton-bodied Dennis Darts were purchased.

LT routes operated are 106, 287, 366, 368. The fleet bears a livery of red, blue and white, and is kept at Thames Road, Silvertown.

Chapel Road, Ilford finds Docklands Minibus 394, a Carlyle bodied example mounted on a Mercedes-Benz 811D. All of the Mercedes-Benz minibuses used on routes 287, 366 and 368 were acquired from fellow group members Red Admiral and Thames Transit.
Richard Godfrey

Following the loss by Cowie Leaside of tendered route 106 during 1996, Docklands Minibus introduced eighteen new Dennis Darts with Plaxton Pointer bodies on the route. 414 is seen at Hackney. Mike Harris

DOCKLANDS MINIBUS

119	D119PTT	Ford Transit			Mellor		B16F	1987	Ex Blue Admiral, 1992		

205–209		Ford Transit			Devon Conversions		C16F	1996			
205	N205YJM	**206**	N206YJM	**207**	N207YJM	**208**	N208YJM	**209**	N209YJM		

367–409		Mercedes-Benz 811D			Carlyle C19		B29F	1991	367–71, 401–9 ex Thames Transit, 1993; 389–400 ex Red Admiral, 1993/4.		
367	H985FTT	**390**	H781GTA	**398**	H789GTA	**403**	H104HDV	**408**	H109HDV		
368	H986FTT	**393**	H784GTA	**399**	H790GTA	**404**	H105HDV	**409**	H110HDV		
370	H988FTT	**394**	H785GTA	**400**	H791GTA	**405**	H106HDV				
371	H989FTT	**395**	H786GTA	**401**	H102HDV	**406**	H107HDV				
389	H180GTA	**397**	H788GTA	**402**	H103HDV	**407**	H108HDV				

410–427		Dennis Dart 9.8SDL3054			Plaxton Pointer		B40F	1996			
410	N410MBW	**414**	N414MBW	**418**	N418MBW	**422**	N422MBW	**426**	N426MBW		
411	N411MBW	**415**	N415MBW	**419**	N419MBW	**423**	N423MBW	**427**	N427MBW		
412	N412MBW	**416**	N416MBW	**420**	N420MBW	**424**	N424MBW				
413	N413MBW	**417**	N417MBW	**421**	N421MBW	**425**	N425MBW				

597	P597YOD	Ford Transit			Devon Conversions		C16F	1996			
644	D644NOD	Ford Transit			Mellor		B16F	1987	Ex Blue Admiral, 1992		
813	E813WDV	Ford Transit			Mellor		B16F	1987	Ex Blue Admiral, 1992		

GREY-GREEN

Cowie Group plc, 53 Stamford Hill, London, N16 5TD

The George Ewer Group of coach companies was taken over by the Cowie Group in 1981, the latter's initial move into bus operation. The first gain into LT tendered operations was the acquisition of route 173 between Stratford and Becontree Heath for which former South Yorkshire Fleetlines were bought. These were painted into an orange, white and brown livery. The now familiar grey and green livery was introduced in 1989. Further LT route gains have progressed since, the major coup being the acquisition of route 24 (Hampstead Heath to Pimlico) in November 1988. This was the first of many central London routes lost by the former LT Buses companies to other operators.

During 1997, new low-floor buses will be purchased for recently retained contract routes 20 and 167 in east London.

LT routes operated are 20, 24, 103, 125, 141, 167, 168, 173, 210, 275, 673, W13. The fleet is painted in grey and green with orange relief; vehicles used on the current Bakerloo Line replacement bus services on behalf of London Underground are in all-over red. The fleet is housed at Barking (Ripple Road) and Stamford Hill (High Road).

The mainstay of the Grey-Green double deck fleet is made up of Volvo Citybuses with Alexander bodywork. 150 is seen here at picturesque Woodford Green in June 1996 on route 235 heading for Leytonstone. Gerald Mead

One of two East Lancs bodied Scanias purchased by Grey-Green in 1988, No.107 is seen at London City Airport on a route recently won by Stagecoach East London.
Colin Lloyd

Below **Grey-Green 172 is one of a batch of former coaches rebodied as double-deckers for almost exclusive use on route 141. Still looking odd with its strangely positioned rear axle and offside emergency exit, it is seen here in High Road, Wood Green in September 1995.**
Mike Harris

Above **Repainted red in 1996 for use on the Bakerloo Line replacement service between Oxford Circus and Elephant & Castle, No.118 is one of 30 Volvo B10Ms received in 1988 for route 24 and gradually being replaced by new Northern Counties bodied Scanias as shown opposite. It is seen in Osidge Lane in October 1996 prior to moving to the Bakerloo Line contract and at Trafalgar Square in November.** Gerald Mead/Russell Upcraft

Right **The latest double deckers in the Grey-Green fleet are these Northern Counties Palatine bodied Scanias. Usually to be found on route 24 between Pimlico and Hampstead Heath, 180 is seen here at Leicester Square Station in August 1996.** Capital Transport

Grey-Green 921 is one of thirteen East Lancashire EL2000 bodied Volvo B10M-55 examples allocated to Stamford Hill garage. These are used mainly on route 210 between Finsbury Park and the Brent Cross Shopping Centre where this one is seen in the summer of 1995. Colin Lloyd

GREY-GREEN

104	E104JYV	Volvo B10M–50	Alexander RV	H43/35F	1987
105	E105JYV	Volvo B10M–50	Alexander RV	H43/35F	1987
107	E107JYV	Scania K92CRB	East Lancashire	H45/31F	1987
108	E108JYV	Scania K92CRB	East Lancashire	H45/31F	1988

109–114

		Scania N112DRB		East Lancashire		H46/29F		1988	
109	E109JYV	111	E111KYN	113	E113KYN
110	E110JYV	112	E112KYN	114	E114KYN

115–144

Volvo B10M–50   Alexander RV   H46/29D   1988   *Red livery
(136 is fitted with an East Lancashire top deck following accident damage)

115*	F115PHM	121	F121PHM	127	F127PHM	133	F133PHM	139	F139PHM
116*	F116PHM	122	F122PHM	128	F128PHM	134	F134PHM	140	F140PHM
117*	F117PHM	123*	F123PHM	129	F129PHM	135	F135PHM	141	F141PHM
118*	F118PHM	124	F124PHM	130	F130PHM	136	F136PHM	142	F142PHM
119*	F119PHM	125*	F125PHM	131	F131PHM	137	F137PHM	143	F143PHM
120	F120PHM	126	F126PHM	132	F132PHM	138	F138PHM	144	F144PHM

145	G145TYT	Volvo B10M–50	Alexander RV	H46/29D	1990
146	G146TYT	Volvo B10M–50	Alexander RV	H46/29D	1990
147	G147TYT	Volvo B10M–50	Alexander RV	H46/29D	1990
148	G148TYT	Volvo B10M–50	Alexander RV	H46/29D	1990

149–158

Volvo B10M–50   Alexander RV   H46/33F   1990

149	G149TYT	151	G151TYT	153	G153TYT	155	H155XYU	157	H157XYU
150	G150TYT	152	G152TYT	154	G154TYT	156	H156XYU	158	H158XYU

159	L159GYL	Scania N113DRB	Northern Counties Palatine	H42/25D	1994
160	L160GYL	Scania N113DRB	Northern Counties Palatine	H42/25D	1994
161	L161GYL	Scania N113DRB	Northern Counties Palatine	H42/25D	1994

163–172

Volvo B10M–61   East Lancs EL2000 (1992)   H44/30D   1985

163	B863XYR	166	B866XYR	170	B870XYR
164	B864XYR	167	B867XYR	171	B871XYR
165	B865XYR	168	B868XYR	172	B872XYR

Acquired from County Bus in 1991 along with route 103, No.413 is one of fifteen Olympians that have remained based at Barking.
Russell Upcraft

178–183

Scania N113DRB — Northern Counties Palatine — H42/25D — 1995/6

178	M178LYP	180	M180LYP	182	N182OYH
179	M179LYP	181	N181OYH	183	N183OYH

401–415

Leyland Olympian ON2R50C13Z4 — Northern Counties — H47/30F — 1990 Ex County, 1991

401	H101GEV	405	H105GEV	409	H109GEV	414	H114GEV
402	H102GEV	406	H106GEV	410	H110GEV	415	H115GEV
403	H103GEV	407	H107GEV	412	H112GEV		
404	H104GEV	408	H108GEV	413	H113GEV		

466	DTG366V	MCW Metrobus DR102/15	MCW	H46/31F	1980 Ex Newport, 1992
467	DTG367V	MCW Metrobus DR102/15	MCW	H46/31F	1980 Ex Newport, 1992
472	DTG372V	MCW Metrobus DR102/15	MCW	H46/31F	1980 Ex Newport, 1993

857–861

Volvo B10M–61 — East Lancashire EL2000 (1992) — B49F — 1985

857	B857XYR	858	B858XYR	859	B859XYR	860	B860XYR	861	B861XYR

912–925

Volvo B10M–55 — East Lancashire EL2000 — B41F — 1990

912	H912XYT	915	H915XYT	918	H918XYT	921	H921XYT	925	H925XYT
913	H913XYT	916	H916XYT	919	H919XYT	922	H922XYT		
914	H914XYT	917	H917XYT	920	H920XYT	923	H923XYT		

926–931

DAF SB220LC550 — Ikarus Citibus — B48F — 1992

926	J926CYL	928	J928CYL	930	J930CYL
927	J927CYL	929	J929CYL	931	J931CYL

934–941

Dennis Dart 9SDL3024 — Plaxton Pointer — B31F — 1993

934	L934GYL	936	L936GYL	938	L938GYL	940	L940GYL
935	L935GYL	937	L937GYL	939	L939GYL	941	L941GYL

950	M950LYR	Dennis Dart 9.8 DL3040	Plaxton Pointer	B40F	1995

952–968

Dennis Dart SLF — Alexander ALX200 — B–F — 1997

952	P952RUL	956	P956RUL	960	P960RUL	964	P964RUL	968	P968RUL
953	P953RUL	957	P957RUL	961	P961RUL	965	P965RUL		
954	P954RUL	958	P958RUL	962	P962RUL	966	P966RUL		
955	P955RUL	959	P959RUL	963	P963RUL	967	P967RUL		

The coach fleet is listed in the London Coach Handbook.

Ilford in August 1995 and Ikarus Citibus 930 plies its trade on its usual haunt, the 167 to Debden. Together with route 20, route 167 has been retained on tender and will be receiving new buses in March 1997. Tony Wilson

Ten Dennis Darts are currently in service with Grey-Green. Seven are allocated daily to route 173 from the Barking garage although, as depicted here, three are used on Sundays on route 275. Cross Road, Woodford finds 935 on its way to Barkingside. Mike Harris

JAVELIN

Service Team Ltd, Eltringham Street, Wandsworth, London, SW18 1TD

Having been successful in winning tenders for both LT Mobility and Surrey County Council Access bus routes, Javelin Coaches have amassed quite a substantial fleet of wheelchair-accessible minibuses. The vehicles for LT routes are all equipped with wheelchair lifts.

LT Mobility Bus routes operated are 904, 905, 926, 938-946, 963, 964, 965, 967, 968, 969, 974-979. Javelin also operate routes 632-638, 640 and 656 on behalf of Surrey County Council. Vehicles on LT routes carry red and white livery, whilst those on Surrey County Council routes carry blue and yellow. These are based respectively at Fulham (Imperial Way) and Ruislip (Glovers Grove, Breakspear Road).

JAVELIN

J514WTW	Mercedes-Benz 709D	Wadham Stringer Wessex	B19FL	1991
J520WTW	Mercedes-Benz 709D	Wadham Stringer Wessex	B20FL	1991
J529WTW	Mercedes-Benz 709D	Wadham Stringer Wessex	B23FL	1991
J530WTW	Mercedes-Benz 709D	Wadham Stringer Wessex	B15FL	1991
K890WPF	Talbot-Pullman Freeway	TBP	B20FL	1993
M190TEV	Mercedes-Benz 709D	WSC Wessex	B20FL	1994
M191TEV	Mercedes-Benz 709D	WSC Wessex	B20FL	1994

Special liveries
Surrey County Council: K890WPF

Many of the west London Mobility routes are now operated by Serviceteam, trading as Javelin Coaches. J529WTW is a Mercedes-Benz 709D with Wadham Stringer Wessex body purchased new in 1991 and, as with all the fleet used on LT routes, a wheelchair lift is fitted. Cromwell Road, Kingston in September 1995 sees the bus on mobility route 940. Geoff Rixon

Unique with the Serviceteam fleet is this TBP Freeway in the livery of Surrey County Council. A rear mounted tail lift is fitted for wheelchair access and the vehicle was seen on route 632 in Sunbury-on-Thames. Colin Lloyd

KENTISH BUS

Kentish Bus Ltd, Invicta House, Armstrong Road, Maidstone, Kent, ME15 6TY

Kentish Bus & Coach was re-named from London Country South East on 27th April 1987, and purchased by the Proudmutual Group, later part of British Bus. British Bus was itself bought out by the Cowie group in June 1996. There was at first considerable success in obtaining London Transport contracts, though some recent results have been less favourable, and this element of work has reduced. From 1st January 1995 some of the London operations have been covered by the newly formed Londonlinks company.

The main livery is primrose yellow with maroon relief, though more recently vehicles for work in Kent have appeared in a livery of green and yellow. Vehicles are based at Battersea and Cambridge Heath, Dartford, Dunton Green and Northfleet. Those at Battersea and Cambridge Heath are used exclusively on LT work, those at Northfleet exclusively on Kent work (other than three Leyland Nationals for Mobility Bus Services), and those at Dartford and Dunton Green on a mixture.

The fleet is due to be renumbered during 1997 into a common series with Maidstone & District and Londonlinks.

Knightsbridge in the summer of 1996 finds Kentish Bus RML2505 working a short journey to Highbury Corner on route 19. One of only a brace of crew routes operated by other than former LT companies, the buses for the 19 are on long term loan from London Transport. Capital Transport

Kentish Bus operate three of their central London routes using forty-one Northern Counties bodied Olympians. 515 is such an example on route 22B in Dalston Lane, Hackney in April 1996.
Mike Harris

The Royal Standard at Blackheath finds Kentish Bus 209 well laden on its way to Lewisham. Route 108 remains unique in being the only bus route to cross the River Thames via the Blackwall Tunnel. The company have been unsuccessful in retaining the route on a recent tender and it will pass to Harris Bus of Grays using new low floor buses in April 1997. Russell Upcraft

Whilst under the control of the Proudmutual group, new vehicles for Kentish Bus received Newcastle registrations. No.563 is a Volvo Olympian new in 1994 with Northern Counties bodywork, and was caught at Woolwich on LT route 96. Mark Lyons

KENTISH BUS

AN186	XPG186T	Leyland Atlantean AN68A/1R	Roe		H43/30F	1979	Ex Londonlinks, 1996
AN196	XPG196T	Leyland Atlantean AN68A/1R	Roe		H43/30F	1979	Ex Londonlinks, 1996

AN203-232   Leyland Atlantean AN68A/1R   Roe   H43/30F   1979/80

AN203	EPH203V	AN211	EPH211V	AN220	EPH220V	AN225	EPH225V
AN208	EPH208V	AN212	EPH212V	AN221	EPH221V	AN231	EPH231V
AN210	EPH210V	AN215	EPH215V	AN224	EPH224V	AN232	EPH232V

AN265-282   Leyland Atlantean AN68B/1R   Roe   H43/30F   1980/81

AN265	KPJ265W	AN271	KPJ271W	AN276	KPJ276W	AN279	KPJ279W
AN269	KPJ269W	AN273	KPJ273W	AN277	KPJ277W	AN282	KPJ282W
AN270	KPJ270W	AN274	KPJ274W	AN278	KPJ278W		

RML2266-2715   AEC Routemaster 9RM   Park Royal   H40/32R   1965-67   Ex London Buses, 1993   Iveco engines

2266	CUV266C	2387	JJD387D	2523	JJD523D	2574	JJD574D
2301	CUV301C	2410	JJD410D	2524	JJD524D	2577	JJD577D
2343	CUV343C	2452	JJD452D	2531	JJD531D	2586	JJD586D
2347	CUV347C	2505	JJD505D	2533	JJD533D	2591	JJD591D
2382	JJD382D	2512	JJD512D	2536	JJD536D	2619	NML619E
2383	JJD383D	2514	JJD514D	2548	JJD548D	2715	SMK715F

9	TIB5905	Leyland Tiger TRCTL11/3RH	Duple 320	C53F	1986	
10	TIB5906	Leyland Tiger TRCTL11/3RH	Duple 320	C51F	1986	
11	XSV689	Leyland Tiger TRCTL11/3RH	Duple 320	C53F	1986	Ex London & Country, 1994
14	TSU644	Leyland Tiger TRCTL11/3R	Plaxton Paramount 3200Exp	C53F	1983	Ex Maidstone & District, 1996
15	YSU895	Leyland Tiger TRCTL11/2R	Duple Laser Express	C50F	1983	Ex Maidstone & District, 1996
21	KBC193	Leyland Tiger TRCTL11/3RH	Berkhof Everest 370	C49FT	1984	
27	OSK776	Leyland Tiger TRCRL11/3RH	Berkhof Everest 370	C49FT	1986	

28	YYB122	Leyland Tiger TRCTL11/3RH	Berkhof Everest 370	C49FT	1986	
29	JSK994	Leyland Tiger TRCTL11/3RH	Berkhof Everest 370	C49FT	1986	
30	TIB5903	Volvo B10M-61	Van Hool Alizée	C53F	1988	Ex Jason, St Mary Cray, 1993
31	TIB5904	Volvo B10M-61	Van Hool Alizée	C53F	1988	Ex Jason, St Mary Cray, 1993
32	HIL2279	Volvo B10M-61	Plaxton Paramount 3500 3	C50F	1988	Ex Wallace Arnold, 1993
35	A11GTA	Volvo B10M-60	Plaxton Paramount 3500 3	C53F	1991	Ex Park, Hamilton, 1994
36	XSV691	Leyland Tiger TRCTL11/3RZ	Plaxton Paramount 3200 3	C53F	1988	Ex London & Country, 1994
38	IIL9168	Leyland Tiger TRCL10/3ARZM	Plaxton Paramount 3200 3	C53F	1989	Ex Moor Dale, Newcastle, 1995
39	IIL9169	Leyland Tiger TRCL10/3ARZM	Plaxton Paramount 3200 3	C53F	1989	Ex Moor Dale, Newcastle, 1995
40	J16AMB	DAF SB3000DKVF601	Van Hool Alizée	C52F	1992	Ex Express Travel, Speke, 1995
41	J17AMB	DAF SB3000DKVF601	Van Hool Alizée	C48FT	1992	Ex Express Travel, Speke, 1995
42	K22AMB	DAF SB3000DKVF601	Van Hool Alizée	C52F	1992	Ex Express Travel, Speke, 1995

87-98

		Dennis Dart 9SDL3002	Duple/Carlyle Dartline	B36F	1990	Ex R&I, London NW10, 1995

87	G217LGK	95	G125RGT	97	G127RGT
93	G123RGT	96	G126RGT	98	G128RGT

112-159

		Dennis Dart 9SDL3034	Northern Counties Countybus Paladin	B35F	1994

112	L112YVK	122	L122YVK	132	L132YVK	142	L142YVK	153	L153YVK
113	L113YVK	123	L123YVK	133	L133YVK	143	L143YVK	154	L154YVK
114	L114YVK	124	L124YVK	134	L134YVK	144	L144YVK	155	L155YVK
115	L115YVK	125	L125YVK	135	L135YVK	145	L145YVK	156	L156YVK
116	L116YVK	126	L126YVK	136	L136YVK	146	L146YVK	157	L157YVK
117	L117YVK	127	L127YVK	137	L137YVK	148	L148YVK	158	L158BFT
118	L118YVK	128	L128YVK	138	L138YVK	149	L149YVK	159	L159BFT
119	L119YVK	129	L129YVK	139	L139YVK	150	L150YVK		
120	L120YVK	130	L130YVK	140	L140YVK	151	L151YVK		
121	L121YVK	131	L131YVK	141	L141YVK	152	L152YVK		

184	P184LKL	Dennis Dart SLF	Plaxton Pointer	B37F	1996
185	P185LKL	Dennis Dart SLF	Plaxton Pointer	B37F	1996

186-191

		Dennis Dart	Plaxton Pointer	B40F	1997

186	P186LKJ	188	P188LKJ	190	P190LKJ
187	P187LKJ	189	P189LKJ	191	P191LKJ

201-212

		Volvo B6	Northern Counties Countybus Paladin	B39F	1994

201	L201YCU	204	L204YCU	207	L207YCU	210	L210YCU
202	L202YCU	205	L205YCU	208	L208YCU	211	L211YCU
203	L203YCU	206	L206YCU	209	L209YCU	212	L212YCU

250-259

		Scania L113CRL	Wright Pathfinder	B43F	1995

250	N250BKK	252	N252BKK	254	N254BKK	256	N256BKK	258	N258BKK
251	N251BKK	253	N253BKK	255	N255BKK	257	N257BKK	259	N259BKK

335	SIB6705	Leyland National 10351A/1R	East Lancs (1992)	B41F	1978	Ex Londonlinks, 1996
336	SIB6706	Leyland National 2 NL106AL11/1R	East Lancs (1992)	B41F	1981	Ex Londonlinks, 1996
337	SIB6707	Leyland National 2 NL106AL11/1R	East Lancs (1992)	B41F	1981	Ex Londonlinks, 1996
338	SIB6708	Leyland National 2 NL106AL11/1R	East Lancs (1992)	B41F	1982	Ex Londonlinks, 1996
345	SIB6715	Leyland National 1051/1R/0402	East Lancs (1993)	B41F	1973	Ex Londonlinks, 1996
346	SIB6716	Leyland National 1051/1R/0402	East Lancs (1993)	B41F	1974	Ex Londonlinks, 1996

348-357

		Leyland National 10351B/1R	East Lancs (1992)	B41F	1978/79

348	SIB1279	350	SIB1281	352	SIB1283	354	SIB1285	356	SIB1287
349	SIB1280	351	SIB1282	353	SIB1284	355	SIB1286	357	SIB1288

361	PDZ6261	Leyland National 10351/1R	East Lancs (1994)	B41F	1977	Ex Londonlinks, 1996
362	PDZ6262	Leyland National 10351/1R	East Lancs (1994)	B41F	1977	Ex Londonlinks, 1996

403-411

		Leyland Lynx LX2R11C15Z4S	Leyland	B49F	1989	Ex Boro'line Maidstone, 1992

403	G36VME	406	G39VME	409	G42VME
404	G37VME	407	G40VME	410	G43VME
405	G38VME	408	G41VME	411	G44VME

413	H813EKJ	Leyland Lynx LX2R11G15Z4S	Leyland	B49F	1991	Ex Boro'line Maidstone, 1992		
414	H814EKJ	Leyland Lynx LX2R11G15Z4S	Leyland	B49F	1991	Ex Boro'line Maidstone, 1992		
415	H815EKJ	Leyland Lynx LX2R11G15Z4S	Leyland	B49F	1991	Ex Boro'line Maidstone, 1992		
416	H816EKJ	Leyland Lynx LX2R11G15Z4S	Leyland	B49F	1991	Ex Boro'line Maidstone, 1992		
417	D155HML	Leyland Lynx LX112TL11ZR1	Leyland	B49F	1987	Ex Boro'line Maidstone, 1992		
419	D157HML	Leyland Lynx LX112TL11ZR1	Leyland	B49F	1987	Ex Boro'line Maidstone, 1992		
445	M445HPF	Optare MetroRider MR17	Optare	B29F	1994	Ex Londonlinks, 1996		
446	M446HPF	Optare MetroRider MR17	Optare	B29F	1994	Ex Londonlinks, 1996		
492	RUF42R	Leyland National 11351/2R		B25DL	1977	Ex London Buses, 1993		
493	THX202S	Leyland National 10351A/2R		B21DL	1978	Ex London Buses, 1993		
494	YYE290T	Leyland National 10351A/2R		B21DL	1979	Ex London Buses, 1993		

514-554
Leyland Olympian ON2R50C13Z4* — Northern Counties — H47/27D — 1990 *514/41/3/4/6-54 are ONCL10/1RZ

514	G514VBB	523	G523VBB	532	G532VBB	541	G541VBB	550	G550VBB
515	G515VBB	524	G524VBB	533	G533VBB	542	G542VBB	551	G551VBB
516	G516VBB	525	G525VBB	534	G534VBB	543	G543VBB	552	G552VBB
517	G517VBB	526	G526VBB	535	G535VBB	544	G544VBB	553	G553VBB
518	G518VBB	527	G527VBB	536	G536VBB	545	G545VBB	554	G554VBB
519	G519VBB	528	G528VBB	537	G537VBB	546	G546VBB		
520	G520VBB	529	G529VBB	538	G538VBB	547	G547VBB		
521	G521VBB	530	G530VBB	539	G539VBB	548	G548VBB		
522	G522VBB	531	G531VBB	540	G540VBB	549	G549VBB		

555	G555VBB	Leyland Olympian ON2R50C13Z4	Northern Counties	H47/27D	1990
556	G556VBB	Leyland Olympian ONCL10/1RZ	Northern Counties	H47/27D	1990

557-565
Volvo Olympian YN2RC16Z4 — Northern Counties Countybus Palatine II — H47/30F — 1994

557	L557YCU	559	L559YCU	562	L562YCU	564	L564YCU
558	L558YVU	561	L561YCU	563	L563YCU	565	L565YCU

601-620
Leyland Olympian ONLXB/1R — Eastern Coach Works — H45/32F* — 1983-85 — * 601 is H44/32F Ex Northumbria, 1990/91

601	WDC219Y	611	A241GHN	614	A244GHN	617	B247NVN	620	C257UAJ
608	CEF231Y	612	A242GHN	615	B245NVN	618	B248NVN		
610	A240GHN	613	A243GHN	616	B246NVN	619	B256RAJ		

631-638
Volvo Citybus B10M-50 — Northern Counties — H45/31F — 1989 — Ex Londonlinks, 1996

631	G631BPH	633	G633BPH	635	G635BPH	637	G637BPH
632	G632BPH	634	G634BPH	636	G636BPH	638	G638BPH

702-709
Volvo Citybus B10M-50 — East Lancs — H49/39F — 1989/90 — Ex North Western, 1996

702	G641CHF	706	G648EKA	708	G659DTJ
703	G642CHF	707	G649EKA	709	G660DTJ

734	F114TML	Volvo Citybus B10M-50	Alexander RV	H47/29D	1989 Ex Boro'line Maidstone, 1992

751-762
Leyland Olympian ONLXB/1RH — Optare — H47/29F — 1988/89 Ex Boro'line Maidstone, 1992

751	E151OMD	754	E154OMD	757	E157OMD	760	E160OMD
752	E152OMD	755	E155OMD	758	E158OMD	761	E161OMD
753	E153OMD	756	E156OMD	759	E159OMD	762	F991UME

764	E164OMD	Volvo Citybus B10M-61	Alexander RV	H47/37F	1988 Ex Boro'line Maidstone, 1992

765-770
Leyland Olympian ON2R50C13Z4 — Northern Counties — H47/30F — 1991 Ex Boro'line Maidstone, 1992

765	H765EKJ	767	H767EKJ	769	H769EKJ
766	H766EKJ	768	H768EKJ	770	H770EKJ

801-808
Optare MetroRider — Optare — B29F — 1996

801	N801BKN	803	N803BKN	805	N805BKN	807	N807BKN
802	N802BKN	804	N804BKN	806	N806BKN	808	N808BKN

836	F393DOA	Talbot Pullman	Talbot	B17FL	1989	Ex Pathfinder, Newark, 1993
841	E31NEF	MCW Metrorider MF154/9	Metro-Cammell-Weymann	DP31F	1988	Ex Londonlinks, 1995
842	E32NEF	MCW Metrorider MF154/9	Metro-Cammell-Weymann	DP31F	1988	Ex Londonlinks, 1995
843	E33NEF	MCW Metrorider MF154/9	Metro-Cammell-Weymann	DP31F	1988	Ex Londonlinks, 1995
844	E34NEF	MCW Metrorider MF154/9	Metro-Cammell-Weymann	DP31F	1988	Ex Londonlinks, 1995
852	N852YKE	Optare MetroRider MR13	Optare	B25F	1995	Ex Londonlinks, 1996
859	F997EKM	MCW Metrorider MF159/2	Metro-Cammell-Weymann	B25F	1988	Ex Boro'line Maidstone, 1992
860	F860LCU	MCW Metrorider MF158/15	Metro-Cammell-Weymann	B31F	1988	Ex Londonlinks, 1995
861	F861LCU	MCW Metrorider MF158/15	Metro-Cammell-Weymann	B31F	1988	Ex Londonlinks, 1995
864	F864LCU	MCW Metrorider MF158/15	Metro-Cammell-Weymann	B31F	1988	Ex Londonlinks, 1995
866	G866TCU	Optare MetroRider MR01	Optare	B31F	1989	Ex Londonlinks, 1995
867	E673DCU	MCW Metrorider MF150/62	Metro-Cammell-Weymann	B21F	1987	Ex Rochester & Marshall, 1990
869	F932LKE	MCW Metrorider MF154/13	Metro-Cammell-Weymann	B33F	1988	Ex Boro'line Maidstone, 1992

871-884

		Talbot Pullman	Talbot	B22F*	1989/90	* 871 is B12FL

871	G871SKE	**876**	G876SKE	**882**	G882SKE
873	G873SKE	**878**	G878SKE	**883**	G883SKE
875	G875SKE	**879**	G879SKE	**884**	G884SKE

886	H886CCU	Optare MetroRider	Optare	B25F	1991	
887	H887CCU	Optare MetroRider	Optare	B25F	1991	
889	H889CCU	Optare MetroRider	Optare	B25F	1991	
890	H890CCU	Optare MetroRider	Optare	B25F	1991	
891	K981KGY	Mercedes-Benz 709D	Dormobile Routemaker	B29F	1993	Ex Transcity, Sidcup, 1993
892	K982KGY	Mercedes-Benz 709D	Dormobile Routemaker	B29F	1993	Ex Transcity, Sidcup, 1993
893	K983KGY	Mercedes-Benz 709D	Dormobile Routemaker	B29F	1993	Ex Transcity, Sidcup, 1993
894	H149NOJ	Mercedes-Benz 709D	Carlyle	B29F	1991	Ex Transcity, Sidcup, 1993
910	D910VCN	Freight Rover Sherpa	Rootes	B8F	1985	Ex Northumbria, 1993

961-975

		Optare MetroRider	Optare	B25F	1991	

961	J961JNL	**970**	J970JNL	**974**	J974JNL
962	J962JNL	**973**	J973JNL	**975**	J975JNL

977	L837MWT	Optare MetroRider MR01	Optare	B31F	1993	Ex Darlington, 1995
978	L838MWR	Optare MetroRider MR01	Optare	B31F	1993	Ex Londonlinks, 1995
980	D340WPE	Ford Transit	Carlyle	B16F	1986	Ex Boro'line Maidstone, 1992
981	D341WPE	Ford Transit	Carlyle	B16F	1986	Ex Boro'line Maidstone, 1992
983	D381WPE	Ford Transit	Carlyle	B16F	1986	Ex Boro'line Maidstone, 1992
984	C524DKO	Ford Transit	Ford	12	1986	Ex Boro'line Maidstone, 1992; crewbus
996	D179CRE	Freight Rover Sherpa	PMT	B16F	1986	Ex Transcity, Sidcup, 1993
997	D417FEH	Freight Rover Sherpa	PMT	B16F	1987	Ex Transcity, Sidcup, 1993
—	J154NKN	Mercedes-Benz 814D	Dormobile	B33F	1992	Ex Crossways Management System, Swanley, 1996

Vehicles on loan

5738	KPJ280W	Leyland Atlantean AN68B/1R	Roe	H43/30F	1981	from Maidstone & District
5742	XPG164T	Leyland Atlantean AN68A/1R	Park Royal	H43/30F	1978	from Maidstone & District
5743	KPJ275W	Leyland Atlantean AN68B/1R	Roe	H43/30F	1981	from Maidstone & District

Previous registrations

A11GTA	H832AHS	PDZ6261	UPB310S	SIB1286	BPL482T	TIB5903	E316OPR
F932LKE	F241JWV,	PDZ6262	UPB313S	SIB1287	BPL483T	TIB5904	E319OPR
217UKL		SIB1279	BPL484T	SIB1288	EPD522V	TIB5905	C261SPC
HIL2279	E300UUB	SIB1280	EPD541V	SIB6705	YPF762T	TIB5906	C264SPC
IIL9168	F714ENE	IB1281	BPL489T	SIB6706	LFR855X	TSU644	FKL174Y
IIL9169	F710ENE	SIB1282	YPL439T	SIB6707	JCK850W	XSV689	C256SPC
JSK994	C153SPB	SIB1283	YPL479T	SIB6708	LFR874X	XSV691	E91OJT
KBC193	B118KPF	SIB1284	YPL445T	SIB6715	TPD176M	YYB122	C152SPB
OSK776	C150SPB	SIB1285	BPL480T	SIB6716	UPE196M	YSU895	A114EPA

Named vehicles
21 Silver Belle, 27 Silver Bullet, 30 Silver Fox, 31 Silver Link

Special liveries
Overall advertisements: AN211/5/74/8, 884
Green Line: 9-11/4, 32/6/8, 40-2
Kentish Express: 21/7, 30/1
White: 35/9
LT Mobility Bus: 492-4
Crossways Business Park: J154NKN

LIMEBOURNE

Q Drive Coaches Ltd., Silverthorne Road, Battersea, London, SW8 3HE

Although both London Buslines and Berks Bucks Bus Company were sold to CentreWest on 20th March 1996, the London coach business operated by Q Drive was retained. At the same time, it was announced that route C10 had been won and it was decided that a bus operation would be set up to operate the route from the Battersea base. The route was taken over in May 1996 using six new Optare MetroRiders in a livery of red with beige skirt and green trim. The livery was the first by a contract operator to utilise an 80% red livery as laid down by LT for buses operating contracts within central London. The company has since been successful in winning tendered route 42 (Liverpool Street to Denmark Hill) which will be taken up in April 1997 from Kentish Bus. This will be operated by new low-floor single deck buses. The operation remains under the control of Q Drive Coaches Ltd of Wokingham in Surrey.

LIMEBOURNE

	Optare Metrorider		Optare	B29F	1996
N201MWW		N203MWW	N205MWW		
N202MWW		N204MWW	N206MWW		

On order
New low floor buses are on order for contract route 42 starting April 1997.

The coach fleet is listed in the London Coach Handbook.

Having made their debut on the London bus scene in 1996 with the winning of tendered route C10, Limebourne have since won route 42 starting in 1997. Representing the new buses introduced in June 1996 is N202MWW seen in Buckingham Palace Road in Victoria in July 1996. As with all recently awarded tendered routes that run into the central London area, red has to form the main part of the livery. Mike Harris

LONDON BUSLINES

Berks Bucks Bus Co Ltd,
Middlesex Business Centre, Bridge Road, Southall, Middlesex, UB2 4AB

In the first round of LT tendering, Len Wright gained route 81 (Hounslow to Slough) from July 1985. Nine former London Fleetlines were acquired and repainted into a yellow and brown livery with London Buslines logos. With the acquisition of more tendered routes, the fleet was expanded with additional Fleetlines from London and Manchester as well as new Leyland Lynx and Mercedes-Benz minibuses. New Dennis Darts were purchased during 1996, improving the age profile of the fleet. On 20th March 1996 Q Drive, which included Berks Bucks and London Buslines, was purchased by CentreWest but at the time of writing remained as a separate company operationally.

LT routes operated are 90, 92, 203, 258, 285, 980-992. Other routes operated are Surrey County Council contracts 218, 404, 427, 436, 441, 446, 461, 551, 666. The fleet bears a livery of yellow and brown with light brown and orange relief; Mobility Buses are yellow and red. The depot is at Southall (Bridge Road).

July 1996 finds London Buslines Leyland Olympian 29 on layover at Richmond Bus Station. One of a batch of seventeen buses bought in 1990, it has bodywork by Northern Counties although both the earlier and later Olympians carry Alexander bodies. Mike Harris

London Buslines operate a few Sunday only routes in Surrey, among which is the 441. Alexander bodied Leyland Olympian 55 freshly repainted into new fleet livery is seen on the Heathrow Perimeter Road on a sunny Sunday afternoon in October 1995. Geoff Rixon

With the winning of tendered route 285, new Plaxton bodied Dennis Darts were painted in this very attractive livery with dedicated route branding. 621 was seen in Kingston during July 1996 soon after entering service. Tony Wilson

The Harrow area Mobility routes are operated by London Buslines using Renault minibuses with Plaxton Beaver bodies. 652 was on layover at Brent Cross Bus Station in July 1995.
Keith Wood

LONDON BUSLINES

24-28

Leyland Olympian ON2R50CZ4 — Alexander RH — H45/29F — 1993

24	L24GAN	25	L25GAN	26	L26GAN	27	L27GAN	28	L28GAN

29-44

Leyland Olympian ON2R50C13Z4 — Northern Counties — H47/30F — 1990

29	H129FLX	32	H132FLX	38	H138FLX	43	H143FLX
30	H130FLX	34	H134FLX	40	H140FLX	44	H144FLX
31	H131FLX	35	H135FLX	41	H141FLX		

46-56

Leyland Olympian ONCL10/1RZ — Alexander RL — H47/28F — 1989

46	G46XLO	49	G49XLO	52	G52XLO	55	G55XLO
47	G47XLO	50	G50XLO	53	G53XLO	56	G56XLO
48	G48XLO	51	G51XLO	54	G54XLO		

131-137

Mercedes-Benz 811D — Plaxton Beaver — B28F — 1991

131	J31KLR	134	J34KLR	136	J36KLR
132	J32KLR	135	J35KLR	137	J37KLR

194	G644YVS	Mercedes-Benz 709D	Reeve Burgess Beaver	B25F	1990

601-632

Dennis Dart SFD412BR5TGD1* — Plaxton Pointer — B37F — 1996 — *601-610 are 9.8SDL3054

601	N601XJM	608	N608XJM	615	N615XJM	622	N622XJM	629	P629CGM
602	N602XJM	609	N609XJM	616	N616XJM	623	N623XJM	630	P630CGM
603	N603XJM	610	N610XJM	617	N617XJM	624	N624XJM	631	P631CGM
604	N604XJM	611	N611XJM	618	N618XJM	625	N625XJM	632	P632CGM
605	N605XJM	612	N612XJM	619	N619XJM	626	N626XJM		
606	N606XJM	613	N613XJM	620	N620XJM	627	P627CGM		
607	N607XJM	614	N614XJM	621	N621XJM	628	P628CGM		

651	K651DBL	Renault-Dodge S75	Plaxton Beaver	B18FL	1992
652	K652DBL	Renault-Dodge S75	Plaxton Beaver	B18FL	1992
653	K653DBL	Renault-Dodge S75	Plaxton Beaver	B18FL	1992
807	D755DLO	Leyland Lynx LX112TL11ZR1S	Leyland	B49F	1987

LONDON CENTRAL

London Central Bus Co Ltd, One Warner Road, London SE5 9LU

London Central was purchased by the Go-Ahead group on 18th October 1994, taking 498 vehicles. These included the largest contingent of Routemasters to be taken by any of the subsidiaries.

Routemasters used on routes 12 and 36 have received branded liveries for these routes. Livery has otherwise remained traditional London red with white relief, accompanied by a stylised fleet logo.

To date, few vehicles have left the fleet; rather, success in tendering has led to an increase in the overall fleet size. The purchase by the Go-Ahead group of London General is to lead to the London Central headquarters moving to the Mitcham base of London General during 1997, though some offices will remain based at Camberwell.

The fleet operates from garages at Bexleyheath, Camberwell, New Cross and Peckham.

RML2275 is unique in having received fixed upper-deck front windows. The dedicated route branding used for route 12 is evident in this shot taken at Trafalgar Square in April 1996. Stephen Madden

At the end of 1995 London Central received seventeen Volvo Olympians with Northern Counties bodywork for use on route 51, gained under LT tendering. NV12 was caught in Woolwich in June 1996. Colin Brown

Below The first batch of Northern Counties-bodied Olympians comprised ten vehicles carrying special livery for use on Docklands Express services. NV4 passes through the Isle of Dogs. Malc McDonald

Contract gains in the early summer of 1995 led to the arrival of nine Volvo Olympians with Alexander bodywork. AV7 cuts a fine sight as it stands at Surrey Quays in June 1996 on its way to Waterloo. Colin Brown

All but one of London's Optare Spectras reside in the London Central fleet. They are normally used on route 3, though this shot of SP23 at Piccadilly Circus in August 1996 demonstrates their occasional use on route 12 on Sundays. Malc McDonald

London Central have one of the ex-West Midlands coach-seated Leyland Titans. T1129, with appropriate addition to its fleetname logo, passes the Elephant & Castle in July 1996. Colin Lloyd

Sixteen Dennis Darts with Plaxton bodywork were delivered to London Central in 1991, forming the start of the DRL class. DRL4, at Woolwich in June 1996, was named 'Uncle Albert'. Colin Brown

Unique in the red London fleets are London Central's eleven Dennis Darts with East Lancs bodywork. DEL9 was seen in Lewisham on their normal haunt, route 484, working out of Camberwell garage. *Colin Lloyd*

LONDON CENTRAL

AN1	VTP258L	Leyland Atlantean AN681/R		Alexander AL		H –/– D	1972	Ex London Buses, 1995; mobile canteen/restroom

AV1–9		Volvo Olympian YN2RC16Z4		Alexander RH		H45/29F	1995	
1	M81MYM	**3**	M83MYM	**5**	M85MYM	**7**	M87MYM	**9**	WLT789
2	M82MYM	**4**	M84MYM	**6**	M86MYM	**8**	M91MYM		

DEL1–11		Dennis Dart 9SDL3034		East Lancs EL2000		B34F	1994	Ex London Buses, 1994
1	L901JRN	**4**	L904JRN	**7**	L907JRN	**10**	L910JRN	
2	L902JRN	**5**	L905JRN	**8**	L908JRN	**11**	L911JRN	
3	L903JRN	**6**	L906JRN	**9**	L909JRN			

DRL1–16		Dennis Dart 9SDL3011		Plaxton Pointer		B34F	1991	Ex London Buses, 1994
1	J601XHL	**5**	J605XHL	**9**	J609XHL	**13**	J613XHL	
2	J602XHL	**6**	J606XHL	**10**	J610XHL	**14**	J614XHL	
3	J603XHL	**7**	J607XHL	**11**	J611XHL	**15**	J615XHL	
4	J604XHL	**8**	J608XHL	**12**	J612XHL	**16**	J616XHL	

L34–261		Leyland Olympian ONLXB/1RH		Eastern Coach Works		H42/26D*	1986–87	* L261 is CH42/26D Ex London Buses, 1994
34	C34CHM	**84**	C84CHM	**89**	C89CHM	**95**	VLT29	**101**	C101CHM
39	C39CHM	**85**	C85CHM	**90**	C90CHM	**96**	C96CHM	**138**	WLT838
40	C40CHM	**88**	C88CHM	**93**	C93CHM	**100**	C100CHM	**261**	2CLT

MA123	G123PGT	Mercedes-Benz 811D		Alexander AM	B28F	1990	Ex London General, 1996
MA129	H429XGK	Mercedes-Benz 811D		Alexander AM	B28F	1991	Ex London General, 1996

Optare StarRiders are becoming a rarity in London. SR48, found at Surrey Quays in June 1996, has clearly emerged from recent repaint, looking as fresh as when it was new.
Colin Brown

MR57u	E633KYW	MCW Metrorider MF150/46			Metro-Cammell-Weymann	B25F	1987	Ex London Buses, 1994	
MR99u	F99YVP	MCW Metrorider MF150/115			Metro-Cammell-Weymann	B23F	1988	Ex London Buses, 1994	
MR103u	F103YVP	MCW Metrorider MF150/115			Metro-Cammell-Weymann	B23F	1988	Ex London Buses, 1994	

MRL136–241		Optare MetroRider MR03			Optare	B26F	1990–93	Ex London Buses, 1994	
136	H136UUA	**156**	H156UUA	**226**	K426HWY	**232**	K432HWY	**238**	K438HWY
137	H137UUA	**157**	H157UUA	**227**	K427HWY	**233**	K433HWY	**239**	K439HWY
138	H138UUA	**158**	H158UUA	**228**	K428HWY	**234**	K434HWY	**240**	K440HWY
139	H139UUA	**159**	H159UUA	**229**	K429HWY	**235**	K435HWY	**241**	K441HWY
140	H140UUA	**224**	K424HWY	**230**	K430HWY	**236**	K436HWY		
155	H155UUA	**225**	K425HWY	**231**	K431HWY	**237**	K437HWY		

NV1–27		Volvo Olympian YN2RV18Z4		Northern Counties Palatine 1		H47/30F	1995		
1	M401RVU	**7**	M407RVU	**13**	N413JBV	**19**	N419JBV	**25**	N425JBV
2	M402RVU	**8**	M408RVU	**14**	N414JBV	**20**	N420JBV	**26**	N426JBV
3	M403RVU	**9**	M409RVU	**15**	WLT815	**21**	N421JBV	**27**	N427JBV
4	M404RVU	**10**	WLT990	**16**	N416JBV	**22**	N422JBV		
5	M405RVU	**11**	N411JBV	**17**	N417JBV	**23**	N423JBV		
6	M406RVU	**12**	N412JBV	**18**	N418JBV	**24**	N424JBV		

NV28–48		Volvo Olympian YN2RV18Z4		Northern Counties Palatine 1		H48/27D	1996		
28	N528LHG	**33**	N533LHG	**38**	WLT688	**43**	N543LHG	**48**	N548LHG
29	N529LHG	**34**	N534LHG	**39**	N539LHG	**44**	N544LHG		
30	N530LHG	**35**	N535LHG	**40**	N540LHG	**45**	N545LHG		
31	N531LHG	**36**	N536LHG	**41**	N541LHG	**46**	N546LHG		
32	N532LHG	**37**	N537LHG	**42**	N542LHG	**47**	N547LHG		

RM9–2151

AEC Routemaster 5RM · Park Royal · H36/28R · 1959–65 · Ex London Buses, 1994

9	VLT9	782	WLT782	1062	62CLT	1305	305CLT	1980	ALD980B
71t	UFF380	787	WLT787	1082	82CLT	1380	380CLT	2022	ALM22B
202	VLT202	868	WLT868	1097	97CLT	1400	400CLT	2051	ALM51B
436	WLT436	872	WLT872	1104	104CLT	1621	KGJ187A	2106	CUV106C
478	WLT478	928	WLT928	1119	119CLT	1666	666DYE	2109	CUV109C
527	WLT527	967	WLT967	1168	168CLT	1797	797DYE	2128	CUV128C
541	WLT541	1002	OYM368A	1174	174CLT	1955	ALD955B	2151	CUV151C
687	WLT687	1033	33CLT	1176	176CLT	1962	ALD962B		
758	WLT758	1058	58CLT	1260	260CLT	1977	ALD977B		

RML883–2733

AEC Routemaster 7RM · Park Royal · H40/32R · 1961–67 · Ex London Buses, 1994; Cummins engines

883	WLT883	2332	CUV332C	2440	JJD440D	2551	JJD551D	2614	NML614E
2270	CUV270C	2335	CUV335C	2454	JJD454D	2554	JJD554D	2629	NML629E
2271	CUV271C	2336	CUV336C	2469	JJD469D	2556	JJD556D	2630	NML630E
2273	CUV273C	2338	CUV338C	2474	JJD474D	2560	JJD560D	2673	SMK673F
2275	CUV275C	2339	CUV339C	2482	JJD482D	2578	JJD578D	2676	SMK676F
2276	CUV276C	2345	CUV345C	2484	JJD484D	2583	JJD583D	2683	SMK683F
2279	CUV279C	2362	CUV362C	2499	JJD499D	2584	JJD584D	2711	SMK711F
2283	CUV283C	2381	JJD381D	2507	JJD507D	2587	JJD587D	2712	SMK712F
2302	CUV302C	2396	JJD396D	2513	JJD513D	2596	JJD596D	2714	SMK714F
2314	CUV314C	2397	JJD397D	2515	JJD515D	2601	NML601E	2733	SMK733F
2318	CUV318C	2400	JJD400D	2529	JJD529D	2604	NML604E		
2327	CUV327C	2411	JJD411D	2539	JJD539D	2613	NML613E		

SP1–25

DAF DB250WB505 · Optare Spectra · H44/27F · 1992–93 · Ex London Buses, 1994

1	K301FYG	7	K307FYG	12	K312FYG	17	170CLT	22	K322FYG
3	K303FYG	8	K308FYG	13	K313FYG	18	18CLT	23	K323FYG
4	K304FYG	9	K309FYG	14	K314FYG	19	19CLT	24	K324FYG
5	K305FYG	10	K310FYG	15	K315FYG	20	20CLT	25	WLT625
6	K306FYG	11	K311FYG	16	K316FYG	21	K321FYG		

SR11–123

Mercedes-Benz 811D · Optare StarRider · B26F · 1988–90 · Ex London Buses, 1994

11	F911YWY	23	F923YWY	29	F29CWY	45	F45CWY	53	F53CWY
14	F914YWY	24	F924YWY	30	F30CWY	47	F47CWY	62	F162FWY
16	F916YWY	25	F925YWY	31	F31CWY	48	F48CWY	63	F163FWY
19	F919YWY	26	F926YWY	41	F41CWY	49	F49CWY	64	F164FWY
21	F921YWY	27	F927YWY	42	F42CWY	51	F51CWY	122	G122SMV
22	F922YWY	28	F928YWY	43	F43CWY	52	F52CWY	123	G123SMV

T75–227

Leyland Titan TNLXB2RRSp · Park Royal · H44/26D* · 1979–80 · * T227 is H44/24D · Ex London Buses, 1994

75t	CUL75V	172t	CUL172V	186	CUL186V
76	CUL76V	173t	CUL173V	191t	CUL191V
164t	CUL164V	185	CUL185V	227	EYE227V

T274–798

Leyland Titan TNLXB2RR · Leyland · H44/24D* · 1981–83 · * T275 is H44/26D · Ex London Buses, 1994

274	GYE274W	384	KYV384X	707	OHV707Y	742	OHV742Y	776	OHV776Y
275	GYE275W	396	KYV396X	709	OHV709Y	747	OHV747Y	778	OHV778Y
292	KYN292X	507	KYV507X	712	OHV712Y	750	OHV750Y	779	OHV779Y
294t	KYN294X	676	OHV676Y	713	OHV713Y	752	OHV752Y	781	OHV781Y
297	KYN297X	677	OHV677Y	715	OHV715Y	755	OHV755Y	782	OHV782Y
310	KYN310X	678	OHV678Y	716	OHV716Y	756	OHV756Y	786	OHV786Y
312	KYV312X	679	OHV679Y	717	OHV717Y	757	OHV757Y	787	OHV787Y
314t	KYV314X	681	OHV681Y	718	OHV718Y	760	OHV760Y	788	OHV788Y
323	KYV323X	683	OHV683Y	720	OHV720Y	763	OHV763Y	790	OHV790Y
325t	KYV325X	685	OHV685Y	722	OHV722Y	764	OHV764Y	792	OHV792Y
327	KYV327X	687	OHV687Y	723	OHV723Y	765	OHV765Y	793	OHV793Y
329	KYV329X	693	OHV693Y	725	OHV725Y	766	OHV766Y	794	OHV794Y
336	KYV336X	694	OHV694Y	732	OHV732Y	767	OHV767Y	795	OHV795Y
352t	KYV352X	696	OHV696Y	735	WLT735	768	OHV768Y	796	OHV796Y
356	KYV356X	701	OHV701Y	736	WLT736	773	OHV773Y	798	OHV798Y
362t	KYV362X	704	OHV704Y	737	OHV737Y	774	OHV774Y		
369t	KYV369X	705	OHV705Y	739	OHV739Y	775	OHV775Y		

T799–1123 Leyland Titan TNLXB2RR Leyland H44/26D* 1983–84 * T803 is O44/26D
Ex London Buses, 1994

799	OHV799Y	913	A913SYE	962	A962SYE	1006	A606THV	1059	A59THX
803	OHV803Y	914	A914SYE	963	A963SYE	1008	A608THV	1060	A60THX
806	OHV806Y	915	A915SYE	964	A964SYE	1009	A609THV	1061	A61THX
808	OHV808Y	916	A916SYE	966	A966SYE	1010	A610THV	1062	A62THX
811	OHV811Y	917	A917SYE	967	A967SYE	1011	A611THV	1063	A63THX
831	A831SUL	919	A919SYE	968	A968SYE	1012	A612THV	1064	A64THX
835	A835SUL	920	A920SYE	969	A969SYE	1014	A614THV	1068	A68THX
839	A839SUL	923	A923SYE	970	A970SYE	1015	A615THV	1070	A70THX
844	A844SUL	924	A924SYE	972	A972SYE	1016	A616THV	1071	A71THX
851	A851SUL	927	A927SYE	973	A973SYE	1017	A617THV	1072	A72THX
852	A852SUL	928	A928SYE	974	A974SYE	1018	A618THV	1073	A73THX
853	A853SUL	929	A929SYE	975	A975SYE	1019	A619THV	1074	A74THX
863	A863SUL	930	A930SYE	977	A977SYE	1020	A620THV	1075	A75THX
864	A864SUL	931	A931SYE	979	A979SYE	1021	A621THV	1078	A78THX
870	A870SUL	932	A932SYE	980	A980SYE	1023	A623THV	1080	B80WUV
871	A871SUL	933	A933SYE	981	A981SYE	1024	A624THV	1082	B82WUV
875	A875SUL	936	A936SYE	982	A982SYE	1033	A633THV	1085	B85WUV
886	A886SYE	937	A937SYE	983	A983SYE	1037	A637THV	1086	B86WUV
887	A887SYE	938	A938SYE	984	A984SYE	1038	A638THV	1087	B87WUV
888	A888SYE	939	A939SYE	985	A985SYE	1040	A640THV	1088	B88WUV
889	A889SYE	940	A940SYE	986	A986SYE	1041	A641THV	1090	B90WUV
890	A890SYE	941	A941SYE	987	A987SYE	1042	A642THV	1094	B94WUV
891	A891SYE	942	A942SYE	989	A989SYE	1043	A643THV	1095	B95WUV
892	A892SYE	943	A943SYE	991	A991SYE	1044	A644THV	1098	B98WUV
893	A893SYE	946	A946SYE	992	A992SYE	1046	A646THV	1102	B102WUV
894	A894SYE	947	A947SYE	993	A993SYE	1047	A647THV	1104	B104WUV
895	A895SYE	948	A948SYE	994	A994SYE	1049	A649THV	1105	B105WUV
897	A897SYE	952	A952SYE	995	A995SYE	1051	A651THV	1107	B107WUV
898	A898SYE	954	A954SYE	997	A997SYE	1053	A653THV	1109	B109WUV
901	A901SYE	955	A955SYE	1000	ALM1B	1054	A654THV	1111	B111WUV
906	A906SYE	956	A956SYE	1001	A601THV	1055	A655THV	1120	B120WUV
907	A907SYE	957	A957SYE	1002	A602THV	1056	A56THX	1123	B123WUV
908	A908SYE	958	A958SYE	1004	A604THV	1057	257CLT		
909	A909SYE	959	A959SYE	1005	A605THV	1058	A58THX		

T1129	WDA4T	Leyland Titan TNLXB1RF	Park Royal	DPH43/29F	1979	Ex London Buses, 1994
TPL10	VLT71	Leyland Tiger TRCTL11/3RH	Plaxton Paramount 3500 2	C49FT	1986	Ex Northern National, 1995

Special liveries
Overall advertisements: T164/72

Named vehicles
DRL1 *Del Boy*, DRL2 *Rodney*, DRL3 *Cassandra*, DRL4 *Uncle Albert*
L93 *Hawk*, L95 *Jaguar*, L261 *Buccaneer*, T803 *Albatross*, T1129 *Harrier*

Previous Registrations

ALM1B	A600THV	N426JBV	N420JBV	WLT736	OHV736Y
KGJ187A	621DYE	N427JBV	N423JBV	WLT789	M89MYM
N416JBV	N421JBV	OYM368A	2CLT	WLT815	N415JBV
N420JBV	N422JBV	UFF380	VLT71	WLT825	K325FYG
N421JBV	N424JBV	VLT9	VLT9, OYM374A	WLT838	C138CHM
N422JBV	N416JBV	VLT29	C95CHM	WLT990	M410RVU
N423JBV	N425JBV	VLT71	C377PCD, PCN762	2CLT	D261FUL
N424JBV	N426JBV	WLT688	N538LHG	170CLY	K371FYG
N425JBV	N427JBV	WLT735	OHV735Y	257CLT	A57THX

LONDON & COUNTRY

London & Country Ltd, Lesbourne Road, Reigate, Surrey, RH2 7LE

Following the sale of London Country South West to the Drawlane Group in February 1988, a new fleetname, London & Country, was adopted from April 1989. Already heavily involved in LT tendered work, the Company acquired a mixed fleet of second-hand Leyland Atlanteans from Manchester, Northern General, Southdown and Strathclyde. The West Surrey operations of Alder Valley were bought in December 1990 and a considerable exchange of vehicles occurred within the newly re-named British Bus plc. In recent years, investment in new buses has been very noticeable. On 18th June 1996, British Bus was purchased by the Cowie Group plc.

LT routes operated are 57, 85, 627, H27, H28, H29, K5, K6, R61, R62. Other routes operated are County Council services in Surrey and commercial services.

The fleet is painted in two-tone green with red relief. Because vehicles used on London Transport work represent only a small part of the company's operations, this listing covers only those buses employed on LT contract routes from the depots at Addlestone, Hounslow and Leatherhead. The full fleet is listed in the *South East Bus Handbook*.

A sole Optare MetroRider was delivered to London & Country during 1996, and is intended to be used on route K6. When photographed in Kingston, however, MR472 was working the 427. Stephen Madden

Route R61 is operated by London & Country with wheelchair accessible vehicles. On layover at Richmond Bus Station in June 1996, Alexander bodied Mercedes-Benz 469 is allocated to Hounslow. Mike Harris

Below **Just two daily double deck LT tendered routes are operated by London & Country, the 57 from Leatherhead garage and, as shown here, route 85 from Addlestone garage. One of 13 East Lancashire bodied Volvo Citybuses bought new in 1989 is seen at Kingston.**
Geoff Rixon

Although now into its thirteenth year of service, LR50 has gained the latest London & Country livery. It is seen passing Wimbledon Station on tendered route 57 which connects Kingston and Streatham. Colin Lloyd

London & Country 908, seen here in Wimbledon, was acquired from Alder Valley in 1990. Many of the original batch of ten Alexander RL bodied Leyland Olympians left the fleet to go to fellow Cowie Group operators during 1996 leaving only four at Leatherhead garage. Colin Lloyd

LONDON & COUNTRY

LT contract vehicles

AN135	UPK135S	Leyland Atlantean AN68A/1R		Park Royal		H43/30F	1978	Ex London Country SW, 1986	
DD1	F201OPD	Dennis Dominator DDA1020		East Lancashire		H51/33F	1988		

DD2–8

		Dennis Dominator DDA1026		East Lancashire		H45/31F	1989		
DD2	F602RPG	**DD4**	F604RPG	**DD6**	F606RPG	**DD8**	F608RPG		
DD3	F603RPG	**DD5**	F605RPG	**DD7**	F607RPG				

DD9	F609RPG	Dennis Dominator DDA1017		East Lancashire		H49/35F	1989		
DMB4	E104JPL	Renault-Dodge S56		Northern Counties		B25F	1988		

DS10–18

		Dennis Dart 9SDL3053		East Lancashire EL2000		B30FL	1995		
DS10	M521MPF	**DS12**	M523MPF	**DS16**	N528SPA	**DS18**	N530SPA		
DS11	M522MPF	**DS13**	M524MPF	**DS17**	N529SPA				

LR 8–75

		Leyland Olympian ONTL11/1R		Roe		H43/29F	1982/4 Ex London Country SW, 1986		
LR8	TPD108X	**LR18**	TPD118X	**LR28**	TPD128X	**LR46**	A146FPG	**LR50**	A150FPG
LR13	TPD113X	**LR27**	TPD127X	**LR29**	TPD129X	**LR48**	A148FPG		

LR74	B274LPH	Leyland Olympian ONTL11/1R	Eastern Coach Works	H43/29F	1985	Ex London Country SW, 1986
LR75	B275LPH	Leyland Olympian ONTL11/1R	Eastern Coach Works	H43/29F	1985	Ex London Country SW, 1986
MM473	P473APJ	Mercedes-Benz 711D	Plaxton Beaver	B27F	1996	
MM474	P474APJ	Mercedes-Benz 811D	Plaxton Beaver	B18FL	1996	
MR472	P472APJ	Optare MetroRider	Optare	B29F	1996	
113	G113TND	Mercedes-Benz 811D	Carlyle C16	B20FL	1990	Ex Bee Line Buzz, 1992
189	G689OHE	Mercedes-Benz 811D	Reeve Burgess Beaver	B20FL	1990	Ex Metrowest, Warley, 1992
190	G690OHE	Mercedes-Benz 811D	Reeve Burgess Beaver	B20FL	1990	Ex Metrowest, Warley, 1992
429	L429CPC	Mercedes-Benz 709D	Danescroft	B27F	1994	
469	N469SPA	Mercedes-Benz 709D	Alexander AM	B22FL	1995	

610–622

		Volvo Citybus B10M–50		East Lancashire		H49/39F	1989		
610	G610BPH	**613**	G613BPH	**616**	G616BPH	**619**	G619BPH	**622**	G622BPH
611	G611BPH	**614**	G614BPH	**617**	G617BPH	**620**	G620BPH		
612	G612BPH	**615**	G615BPH	**618**	G618BPH	**621**	G621BPH		

901	F571SMG	Leyland Olympian ONLXB/1RZ	Alexander RL	H47/32F	1988	Ex Alder Valley, 1990
907	F577SMG	Leyland Olympian ONLXB/1RZ	Alexander RL	H47/32F	1988	Ex Alder Valley, 1990
908	F578SMG	Leyland Olympian ONLXB/1RZ	Alexander RL	H47/32F	1988	Ex Alder Valley, 1990
910	F580SMG	Leyland Olympian ONLXB/1RZ	Alexander RL	H47/32F	1988	Ex Alder Valley, 1990

LONDON GENERAL

London General Transport Services Ltd, 25 Raleigh Gardens, Mitcham, Surrey, CR4 3NS

London General was purchased by a management-led team on 2nd November 1994, taking 636 vehicles, and thus becoming the largest of the privatised London companies. In May 1996 the company was in turn purchased by the Go-Ahead group, and some rationalisation with London Central is planned in the coming months at the organisational level.

Traditional London livery of red with white relief has been retained, accompanied by a fleetname logo incorporating a vertical orange stripe, similar to that deployed for the VN class on Clapham Omnibus route 88 since 1993. An unusual event in the summer 1996 was the operation of an open-top sightseeing service in the Medway Towns. Major orders are now being delivered, chiefly in association with the retention of LT contracts in the Sutton area.

The fleet operates from garages at Battersea Bridge, Merton, Putney, Stockwell, Sutton and Waterloo. Major maintenance of Battersea Bridge and Waterloo vehicles is undertaken at Stockwell.

Putney's Metrobuses are used on route 74 during the week. M848 has just arrived at Baker Street, the northern terminus of the route, in May 1996. Note that London General blinds qualify this point as serving Madame Tussaud's. Colin Brown

Left **Almost half of the VC class of Volvos with Northern Counties bodywork have received cherished registrations. VC4, seen at Parliament Square, is one of three with high-back seating in the upper saloon. Three others have high-back seating throughout.** Colin Lloyd

Centre **The VN class of Volvo single-deckers with Northern Counties bodywork is used from Stockwell garage on route 88, marketed as 'The Clapham Omnibus'. All carry DVLC select registrations which reflect the initials of the Managing Director. VN11 crosses into Whitehall on a southbound journey in July 1996.** Stephen Madden

Bottom **DR152, a Dennis Dart with Plaxton bodywork, demonstrates the Streetline marketing name used by London General for operations with smaller single-deckers.** Stephen Madden

London General's RMLs are shared between Putney garage and the Waterloo site.
RML2725, from the latter allocation, demonstrates the route branding used for route 11, on
which the type is used on Mondays to Fridays, as it rounds Trafalgar Square in July 1996.
Stephen Madden

Leyland National 2 vehicles used on the Red Arrow network were all rebuilt to Greenway
specification by East Lancs during the earlier part of the decade. GLS439 approaches the
terminus at Waterloo on route 505. Stephen Madden

The first of fifteen Marshall midibuses ordered by London General for contract routes, ML5 entered service in October 1996 from Putney garage on route C3, and was caught at Clapham Junction during its first few days in service. Colin Lloyd

Bearing a registration nearly thirty years older than itself, DW66 presented itself in Hackbridge on route 393. This is a Dennis Dart of 1991 with Wright bodywork. Unlike most other former LBL subsidiaries, London General eschewed Irish registrations for Wright-bodied vehicles, on grounds of security. Richard Godfrey

Above **M241 was converted to open-top in 1996 and painted in traditionally-based General livery for use on a tourist route in the Medway Towns. After the close of the season, it appeared on Surrey heritage route 70D, as depicted at Burford Bridge in September 1996.** Malc McDonald

Above left **London General have a good share of the Optare MetroRiders which joined the LBL fleet in the early 1990s. MRL183 pauses in Merton in July 1996 en route from New Malden to Pollards Hill Estate.** Colin Brown

Left **One of two Mercedes-Benz 709D vehicles with Reeve Burgess bodywork, MT5 is normally used on Riverside Hospital contract services, though when photographed it was at Wimbledon with a rather apologetically makeshift destination display.** Colin Lloyd

LONDON GENERAL

DMS2257t OJD257R		Leyland Fleetline FE30ALRSp		Metro-Cammell-Weymann	H44/24D	1977	Ex London Buses, 1994	
DMS2290t THX290S		Leyland Fleetline FE30ALRSp		Metro-Cammell-Weymann	H44/24D	1977	Ex London Buses, 1994	

DMS2347-2499 Leyland Fleetline FE30ALRSp   Park Royal   H44/24D   1977   Ex London Buses, 1994

2347t	OJD347R	**2397t**	OJD397R	**2413t**	OJD413R	**2476t**	THX476S	**2489t**	THX489S

All DMS vehicles carry the unofficial class code DMT

DPL1-16 Dennis Dart 9SDL3053   Plaxton Pointer   B35F   1995

1	M201EGF	**5**	M205EGF	**9**	M209EGF	**13**	M213EGF
2	M202EGF	**6**	M206EGF	**10**	M210EGF	**14**	M214EGF
3	M203EGF	**7**	M207EGF	**11**	M211EGF	**15**	M215EGF
4	M204EGF	**8**	M208EGF	**12**	M212EGF	**16**	M216EGF

DR32-153 Dennis Dart 8.5SDL3003*   Plaxton Pointer   B28F   1991/92 *DRL149-53 are 8.5SDL3015
Ex London Buses, 1994

32	WLT532	**37**	H537XGK	**44**	H544XGK	**49**	H549XGK	**150**	K150LGO
33	H533XGK	**38**	H538XGK	**45**	H545XGK	**50**	H550XGK	**151**	K151LGO
34	H534XGK	**39**	H539XGK	**46**	46CLT	**51**	H551XGK	**152**	K152LGO
35	H835XGK	**41**	H541XGK	**47**	H547XGK	**52**	H552XGK	**153**	K153LGO
36	H536XGK	**43**	H543XGK	**48**	H548XGK	**149**	K149LGO		

DRL53-73 Dennis Dart 9SDL3016   Plaxton Pointer   B34F+16   1992   Ex London Buses, 1994

53	K853LGN	**58**	K858LGN	**63**	K863LGN	**68**	K868LGN	**73**	K873LGN
54	K854LGN	**59**	K859LGN	**64**	K864LGN	**69**	K869LGN		
55	K855LGN	**60**	K860LGN	**65**	K865LGN	**70**	K870LGN		
56	K856LGN	**61**	K861LGN	**66**	K866LGN	**71**	K871LGN		
57	K857LGN	**62**	K862LGN	**67**	K867LGN	**72**	K872LGN		

DRL74-95 Dennis Dart 9SDL3024   Plaxton Pointer   B32F   1993   Ex London Buses, 1994

74	K574MGT	**79**	K579MGT	**84**	K584MGT	**89**	K589MGT	**94**	K767OGK
75	K575MGT	**80**	K580MGT	**85**	K585MGT	**90**	K590MGT	**95**	WLT395
76	K576MGT	**81**	K581MGT	**86**	K586MGT	**91**	K591MGT		
77	K577MGT	**82**	K582MGT	**87**	K587MGT	**92**	K592MGT		
78	K578MGT	**83**	K583MGT	**88**	K588MGT	**93**	K593MGT		

DW44-58 Dennis Dart 8.5SDL3003   Wright Handybus   B30F   1990-91   Ex London Buses, 1994

44	JDZ2344	**47**	WLT470	**50**	JDZ2350	**53**	JDZ2353	**56**	JDZ2356
45	545CLT	**48**	WLT548	**51**	JDZ2351	**54**	JDZ2354	**57**	JDZ2357
46	WLT346	**49**	JDZ2349	**52**	352CLT	**55**	JDZ2355	**58**	JDZ2358

DW66-161 Dennis Dart 8.5SDL3015*   Wright Handybus   B29F   1991-93 * DW66-70 are 8.5SDL3003
Ex London Buses, 1994

66	166CLT	**69**	H369XGC	**128**	K128LGO	**131**	K131LGO	**161**	NDZ3161
67	H367XGC	**70**	H370XGC	**129**	K129LGO	**132**	K132LGO		
68	H368XGC	**127**	K127LGO	**130**	K130LGO	**160**	NDZ3160		

GLS1-506 Leyland National 2 NL106AL11/2R East Lancs Greenway   B24D+46   1981 Rebuilt 1992-4; ex London Buses, 1994 *GLS448/86/91/6/505 are B38D

1	GUW466W	**450**	GUW450W	**471**	GUW471W	**483**	83CLT	**499**	WLT599
438	GUW438W	**452**	GUW452W	**473**	GUW473W	**486**	186CLT	**500**	GUW500W
439	GUW439W	**455**	GUW455W	**474**	GUW474W	**487**	WLT487	**501**	GUW501W
440	GUW440W	**459**	GUW459W	**476**	GUW476W	**490**	GUW490W	**502**	GUW502W
442	GUW442W	**460**	GUW460W	**477**	GUW477W	**491**	GUW491W	**505**	GUW505W
443	WLT843	**463**	GUW463W	**478**	GUW478W	**492**	GUW492W	**506**	GUW506W
446	GUW446W	**467**	WLT467	**479**	GUW479W	**493**	GUW493W		
448	WLT648	**468**	GUW468W	**480**	VLT180	**496**	WLT696		
449	GUW449W	**469**	GUW469W	**481**	GUW481W	**498**	WLT598		

LDP1-17 Dennis Dart SFD112BR1TGW1   Plaxton Pointer   B32F   1996

1	P501RYM	**5**	P505RYM	**9**	P509RYM	**13**	P513RYM	**17**	P517RYM
2	P502RYM	**6**	P506RYM	**10**	P510RYM	**14**	P514RYM		
3	P503RYM	**7**	P507RYM	**11**	P511RYM	**15**	P515RYM		
4	P504RYM	**8**	P508RYM	**12**	P512RYM	**16**	P516RYM		

LDP18-44   Dennis Dart SFD212BR1TGW1   Plaxton Pointer B36F   1996

18	P718RYL	24	P724RYL	30	P730RYL	36	P736RYL	42	P742RYL
19	P719RYL	25	P725RYL	31	P731RYL	37	P737RYL	43	P743RYL
20	P720RYL	26	P726RYL	32	P732RYL	38	P738RYL	44	P744RYL
21	P721RYL	27	P727RYL	33	P733RYL	39	P739RYL		
22	P722RYL	28	P728RYL	34	P734RYL	40	P740RYL		
23	P723RYL	29	P729RYL	35	P735RYL	41	P741RYL		

M11-202   MCW Metrobus DR101/9*   Metro-Cammell-Weymann   H43/28D*   1978-79   Ex London Buses, 1994
*M11-47 are DR101/8; M171 is O43/27F

11	WYW11T	76	WYW76T	164	BYX164V	177	BYX177V	197	197CLT
45	WYW45T	120	BYX120V	165	BYX165V	188	188CLT	198	SGK374V
47	WYW47T	144	BYX144V	171	BYX171V	190	BYX190V	201	BYX201V
56	WYW56T	156	BYX156V	174	BYX174V	191	BYX191V	202t	BYX202V
61	WYW61T	158	BYX158V	176	BYX176V	196	BYX196V		

M171 carries the unofficial fleet number OM171.

M207-502   MCW Metrobus DR101/12   Metro-Cammell-Weymann   H43/28D*   1980   Ex London Buses, 1994
*M241 is O43/28F

207	BYX207V	254	BYX254V	286	BYX286V	350	GYE350W	430	GYE430W
209t	BYX209V	255	BYX255V	287	BYX287V	351	GYE351W	431	GYE431W
211	BYX211V	256	BYX256V	288	BYX288V	354	GYE354W	433	GYE433W
212	BYX212V	257	BYX257V	289	BYX289V	355	GYE355W	435	GYE435W
214	BYX214V	258	BYX258V	292	BYX292V	357	GYE357W	447	GYE447W
216	BYX216V	259	BYX259V	293	BYX293V	359	GYE359W	457	GYE457W
219	BYX219V	260	BYX260V	295	BYX295V	361	GYE361W	463	WLT463
224	BYX224V	261	BYX261V	297	BYX297V	375	GYE375W	466	GYE466W
226	BYX226V	262	BYX262V	302	BYX302V	379	WLT379	471	GYE471W
228	BYX228V	265	BYX265V	303	BYX303V	386	GYE386W	472	GYE472W
231	BYX231V	267	BYX267V	307	BYX307V	392	GYE392W	475	GYE475W
235	BYX235V	269	BYX269V	318	EYE318V	401	GYE401W	476	GYE476W
237	BYX237V	270	BYX270V	320	EYE320V	404	GYE404W	477	GYE477W
239	BYX239V	271t	BYX271V	321	EYE321V	405	GYE405W	479	VLT179
241	BYX241V	273	BYX273V	323	EYE323V	408	GYE408W	480	GYE480W
242	BYX242V	274	BYX274V	325	EYE325V	411	GYE411W	483	GYE483W
244	BYX244V	275	BYX275V	331	EYE331V	412	GYE412W	484	GYE484W
246	BYX246V	278	78CLT	333	EYE333V	416	GYE416W	488	GYE488W
249	BYX249V	279	BYX279V	334	EYE334V	420	GYE420W	490	GYE490W
252	BYX252V	284	VLT284	348	GYE348W	423	GYE423W	502	GYE502W

M209/71 are based in Plymouth for driver training work. M241 carries the unofficial fleet number OM241.

M513-794   MCW Metrobus DR101/14   Metro-Cammell-Weymann   H43/28D   1981-82   Ex London Buses, 1994

513	GYE513W	546	GYE546W	607	KYO607X	695	KYV695X	779	KYV779X
514	GYE514W	556	GYE556W	662	KYV662X	706	KYV706X	794	KYV794X
516	GYE516W	566	GYE566W	667	KYV667X	725	KYV725X		
527	GYE527W	589	GYE589W	668	KYV668X	760	KYV760X		
532	GYE532W	597	GYE597W	670	KYV670X	763	KYV763X		
542	542CLT	606	KYO606X	690	KYV690X	769	KYV769X		

M806-953   MCW Metrobus DR101/16   Metro-Cammell-Weymann   H43/28D   1983   Ex London Buses, 1994

806	OJD806Y	826	OJD826Y	852	OJD852Y	897	A897SUL	926	A926SUL
807	OJD807Y	828	OJD828Y	853	SGC671Y	900	A900SUL	931	A931SUL
808	OJD808Y	830	OJD830Y	854	OJD854Y	902	A902SUL	933	A933SUL
811	OJD811Y	833	OJD833Y	855	OJD855Y	904	A904SUL	940	A940SUL
812	OJD812Y	834	OJD834Y	862	OJD862Y	905	A905SUL	942	A942SUL
814	OJD814Y	837	OJD837Y	867	OJD867Y	907	A907SUL	944	A944SUL
816	OJD816Y	838	OJD838Y	868	OJD868Y	908	A908SUL	946	A946SUL
817	OJD817Y	842	OJD842Y	870	OJD870Y	909	A909SUL	947	A947SUL
818	OJD818Y	845	OGK708Y	871	OJD871Y	913	A913SUL	949	A949SUL
820	OJD820Y	846	OJD846Y	873	OJD873Y	914	A914SUL	953	A953SUL
821	OJD821Y	847	OJD847Y	877	OJD877Y	918	A918SUL		
822	OJD822Y	848	OJD848Y	880	OJD880Y	922	A922SUL		
823	OJD823Y	849	OJD849Y	888	OJD888Y	923	A923SUL		

M965-1440

MCW Metrobus DR101/17* Metro-Cammell-Weymann H43/28D* 1984-86 Ex London Buses, 1994
*M1046/55 are DR101/19; M1432/5/40 are DPH43/28D

965	A965SYF	1107	B107WUL	1225	B225WUL	1306	C306BUV	1388	C388BUV
970	A970SYF	1108	B108WUL	1226	B226WUL	1311	C311BUV	1389	89CLT
975	A975SYF	1177	B177WUL	1230	B230WUL	1315	C109NGH	1391	C391BUV
976	A976SYF	1180	B180WUL	1232	B232WUL	1337	C337BUV	1410	C410BUV
977	A977SYF	1196	B196WUL	1235	B235WUL	1347	C347BUV	1411	C411BUV
978	A978SYF	1203	B203WUL	1237	B237WUL	1357	C357BUV	1432	WLT432
983	A983SYF	1206	B206WUL	1241	B241WUL	1364	C364BUV	1433	C433BUV
991	A991SYF	1211	B211WUL	1264	B264WUL	1370	C370BUV	1434	WLT434
992	A992SYF	1215	B215WUL	1268	B268WUL	1371	C371BUV	1435	435CLT
1002	A702THV	1220	B220WUL	1301	B301WUL	1372	772DYE	1436	VLT136
1005	A705THV	1222	B222WUL	1302	B302WUL	1373	C373BUV	1440	C440BUV
1046	VLT46	1223	B223WUL	1304	304CLT	1386	C386BUV		
1055	A755THV	1224	B224WUL	1305	B305WUL	1387	C387BUV		

MA113-134

Mercedes-Benz 811D Alexander AM B28F 1990/91 Ex London Buses, 1994

113	G113PGT	126	H426XGK	130	H430XGK	133	H433XGK
121	G121PGT	127	H427XGK	131	H431XGK	134	H434XGK
125	H425XGK	128	H428XGK	132	H432XGK		

ML1-15

Marshall Minibus Marshall B29F 1996/7

1	P501HEG	4	P504HEG	7	P407KAV	10	P410KAV	13	P403KAV
2	P502HEG	5	P505HEG	8	P408KAV	11	P401KAV	14	P404KAV
3	P503HEG	6	P506HEG	9	P409KAV	12	P402KAV	15	P405KAV

MRL135-223

Optare MetroRider MR03 Optare B26F 1990-93 Ex London Buses, 1994

135	H135TGO	183	H683YGO	190	H690YGO	197	J697CGK	204	J704CGK
177	VLT277	184	H684YGO	191	J691CGK	198	698DYE	205	J705CGK
178	H678YGO	185	H685YGO	192	J692CGK	199	J699CGK	206	J706CGK
179	H679YGO	186	H686YGO	193	J693CGK	200	J710CGK	207	J707CGK
180	H680YGO	187	H687YGO	194	J694CGK	201	J701CGK	208	J708CGK
181	H681YGO	188	H688YGO	195	J695CGK	202	J702CGK	209	J709CGK
182	H682YGO	189	H689YGO	196	J696CGK	203	J703CGK	223	K223MGT

MT3	F393DHL	Mercedes-Benz 709D	Reeve Burgess Beaver	B20FL	1988	Ex London Buses, 1994
MT5	F395DHL	Mercedes-Benz 709D	Reeve Burgess Beaver	B20FL	1988	Ex London Buses, 1994

NV101-142

Volvo Olympian Nothern Counties Palatine H–D 1997

101	P901RYO	110	P910RYO	119		128		137	
102	P902RYO	111	P911RYO	120		129		138	
103	P903RYO	112	P912RYO	121		130		139	
104	P904RYO	113	P913RYO	122		131		140	
105	P905RYO	114	P914RYO	123		132		141	
106	P906RYO	115	P915RYO	124		133		142	
107	P907RYO	116		125		134			
108	P908RYO	117		126		135			
109	P909RYO	118		127		136			

RM994	WLT994	AEC Routemaster 5RM	Park Royal	H36/28R	1961	Ex London Buses, 1994

RML887-2752

AEC Routemaster 7RM Park Royal H40/32R* 1961-68 Ex London Buses 1994
Iveco engines *RML2516 is H40/32RD and carries the unofficial fleet number DRM2516

887	WLT887	2360	CUV360C	2461	JJD461D	2570	JJD570D	2640	NML640E
889	WLT889	2361	CUV361C	2465	JJD465D	2575	JJD575D	2644	NML644E
894	WLT894	2363	CUV363C	2466	JJD466D	2576	JJD576D	2648	NML648E
899	WLT899	2364	JJD364D	2472	JJD472D	2580	JJD580D	2654	NML654E
2262	CUV262C	2371	JJD371D	2475	JJD475D	2590	JJD590D	2669	SMK669F
2263	CUV263C	2376	JJD376D	2502	JJD502D	2593	JJD593D	2680	SMK680F
2290	CUV290C	2385	JJD385D	2516	WLT516	2605	NML605E	2693	SMK693F
2297	CUV297C	2389	JJD389D	2517	JJD517D	2606	NML606E	2725	SMK725F
2305	CUV305C	2398	JJD398D	2520	JJD520D	2612	NML612E	2732	SMK732F
2316	CUV316C	2403	JJD403D	2535	JJD535D	2615	NML615E	2736	SMK736F
2317	CUV317C	2412	JJD412D	2540	JJD540D	2618	NML618E	2745	SMK745F
2321	CUV321C	2422	JJD422D	2543	JJD543D	2626	NML626E	2752	SMK752F
2342	CUV342C	2441	JJD441D	2564	JJD564D	2631	NML631E		
2358	CUV358C	2453	JJD453D	2568	JJD568D	2637	NML637E		

SC1t	D585OOV	Freight Rover Sherpa		Carlyle Citybus	B6F	1987	Ex London Buses, 1994	

VC1-39		Volvo Citybus B10M-50		Northern Counties	H47/35D*	1989-91	* VC1-3 are DPH45/35D, VC4-6 are H45/35D Ex London Buses, 1994

#		#		#		#		#	
1	101CLT	10	G110NGN	19	619DYE	28	528CLT	37	WLT837
2	G102NGN	11	WLT311	20	WLT920	29	229CLT	38	G138PGK
3	WLT803	12	312CLT	21	621DYE	30	G130PGK	39	839DYE
4	WLT474	13	G113NGN	22	G122NGN	31	G131PGK		
5	G105NGN	14	614DYE	23	23CLT	32	G132PGK		
6	VLT60	15	G115NGN	24	G124NGN	33	G133PGK		
7	G107NGN	16	G116NGN	25	125CLT	34	G134PGK		
8	G108NGN	17	G117NGN	26	G126NGN	35	G135PGK		
9	G109NGN	18	WLT818	27	G127NGN	36	836DYE		

VN1-13		Volvo B10B-58		Northern Counties Paladin	B40D	1993	Ex London Buses, 1994

#		#		#		#		#	
1	K100KLL	4	K4KLL	7	K70KLL	10	K10KLL	13	K13KLL
2	K2KLL	5	K5KLL	8	K8KLL	11	K11KLL		
3	K3KLL	6	K6KLL	9u	K9KLL	12	K12KLL		

VWL1	N101HGO	Volvo B6LE		Wright Crusader	B36F	1995

Previous registrations

C109NGH C315BUV, VLT15	WLT474 G104NGN	125CLT G125NGN
K767OGK K594MGT, WLT994	WLT487 GUW487W	166CLT H366XGC
OGK708Y OJD845Y, 545CLT	WLT516 JJD516D	186CLT GUW486W
SGC671Y OJD853Y, VLT53	WLT532 H532XGK	188CLT BYX188V
SGK374V BYX198V, VLT98	WLT548 JDZ2348	197CLT BYX197V
VLT46 A746THV	WLT598 GUW498W	229CLT G129PGK
VLT60 G106NGN	WLT599 GUW499W	304CLT B304WUL
VLT136 C436BUV	WLT648 GUW448W	312CLT G112NGN
VLT179 GYE479W	WLT696 GUW496W	352CLT JDZ2352
VLT180 GUW480W	WLT803 G103NGN	435CLT C435BUV
VLT277 H677YGO	WLT818 G118NGN	528CLT G128PGK
VLT284 BYX284V	WLT837 G137PGK	542CLT GYE542W
WLT311 G111NGN	WLT843 GUW443W	545CLT JDZ2345
WLT346 JDZ2346	WLT920 G120NGN	614DYE G114NGN
WLT379 GYE379W	WLT994 WLT994, VLT89	619DYE G119NGN
WLT395 K595MGT	23CLT G123NGN	621DYE G121NGN
WLT432 C432BUV	46CLT H546XGK	698DYE J698CGK
WLT434 C434BUV	78CLT BYX278V	772DYE C372BUV
WLT463 GYE463W	83CLT GUW483W	836DYE G136PGK
WLT467 GUW467W	89CLT C389BUV	839DYE J139DGF
WLT470 JDZ2347	101CLT G101NGN	

Named vehicles
GLS438 *City of London*, M1440 *The General*

Special liveries
Traditional London General livery: M171, M241, M978, M1432/40, RML2516
Overall advertisements: M202, M978, M1389

LONDONLINKS

Londonlinks Ltd, Invicta House, Armstrong Road, Maidstone, Kent, ME15 6TY

Londonlinks was established by the British Bus Group in January 1995 to take over most of the London-based operations of Kentish Bus and London & Country. In April 1996, the former Kentish Bus contracts, based at Dunton Green, passed back to that company. Administration, which from the start was under the wing of Kentish Bus at Northfleet, moved to Maidstone in October 1995 when that aspect was merged with Maidstone & District. In June 1996 control of British Bus interests passed to the Cowie group.

Vehicles operate in a livery of light green with dark green and red relief, and are based at depots in Croydon and Walworth. In addition, some Kentish Bus vehicles based at Dunton Green carry Londonlinks livery.

Londonlinks acquired a batch of thirteen Northern Counties bodied Volvo's from London & Country during 1995 and these are allocated to Croydon and Dunton Green garages. July 1996 finds 641 on route 57 at Kingston. Geoff Rixon

Bought new in 1992 by Transcity of Sidcup for LT tendered route 286, this Dart has subsequently been repainted twice and now carries Londonlinks livery as shown at East Croydon on route 407 in the summer of 1996.
Colin Lloyd

Following the splitting of Londonlinks from London & Country in 1995, a batch of thirty-six Volvo Citybuses with East Lancashire bodies was transferred to cover routes running from Croydon and Walworth garages. October 1996 sees 671 at Elephant & Castle on route 176 heading south to Penge. Stephen Madden

Route 367 is operated by Londonlinks between Bromley North Station and West Croydon using seven Plaxton Beaver bodied Mercedes-Benz 811Ds allocated to Croydon garage. 430 is seen here near Bromley South Station.
Mike Harris

Very few Leyland Atlanteans remain in service in the London area although Londonlinks retain eight examples. AN262 is the usual bus used in Croydon on the special Bingo shuttle route 600 as seen here in April 1996 at East Croydon. Colin Lloyd

Most of the Volvo Citybuses with Alexander bodywork which arrived with Kentish Bus from Boro'line Maidstone in 1992 have now been moved over to Londonlinks to replace Leyland Titans at Walworth. No.721, the first of the batch, negotiates the Elephant & Castle traffic system.
Stephen Madden

The newest double deckers in the Londonlinks fleet are a batch of Volvo Olympians with East Lancashire bodies acquired from London & Country in 1995. Number 687 in Croydon High Street works route 400 on its way to Caterham-on-the-Hill.
Colin Lloyd

Route 407 operates between Sutton and Caterham Valley using up to ten buses, both Optare MetroRiders and Dennis Darts from Croydon garage. A sunny South Croydon finds MetroRider 451, one of a batch of fourteen bought new in 1994. Russell Upcraft

LONDONLINKS

AN172	XPG172T	Leyland Atlantean AN68A/1R	Park Royal		H43/30F	1979	Ex London & Country, 1995
AN174	XPG174T	Leyland Atlantean AN68A/1R	Park Royal		H43/30F	1979	Ex London & Country, 1995
AN192	XPG192T	Leyland Atlantean AN68A/1R	Park Royal		H43/30F	1979	Ex Kentish Bus, 1996
AN262	KPJ262W	Leyland Atlantean AN68B/1R	Roe		H43/30F	1981	Ex Maidstone & District, 1995
AN264	KPJ264W	Leyland Atlantean AN68B/1R	Roe		H43/30F	1981	Ex Maidstone & District, 1995
AN268	KPJ268W	Leyland Atlantean AN68B/1R	Roe		H43/30F	1981	Ex Kentish Bus, 1996
AN272	KPJ272W	Leyland Atlantean AN68B/1R	Roe		H43/30F	1981	Ex Kentish Bus, 1995
AN289	KPJ289W	Leyland Atlantean AN68B/1R	Roe		H43/30F	1981	Ex Maidstone & District, 1995

LR11-26

		Leyland Olympian ONTL11/1R	Roe		H43/29F	1982	Ex London & Country, 1995

12	TPD112X	**20**	TPD120X	**22**	TPD122X	**25**	TPD125X
19	TPD119X	**21**	TPD121X	**24**	TPD124X	**26**	TPD126X

100	J220HGY	Dennis Dart 9SDL3011	Plaxton Pointer	B35F	1992	Ex Kentish Bus, 1996
101	J221HGY	Dennis Dart 9SDL3011	Plaxton Pointer	B35F	1992	Ex Kentish Bus, 1996
160	M160SKR	Dennis Dart 9SDL3053	Plaxton Pointer	B35F	1995	
161	M161SKR	Dennis Dart 9SDL3053	Plaxton Pointer	B35F	1995	
162	M162SKR	Dennis Dart 9SDL3053	Plaxton Pointer	B35F	1995	
163	M163SKR	Dennis Dart 9SDL3053	Plaxton Pointer	B35F	1995	

311-316

		Leyland Lynx LX2RG15Z4S	Leyland		B49F	1990	Ex London & Country, 1995

311	G311DPA	**313**	G313DPA	**315**	G315DPA	
312	G312DPA	**314**	G314DPA	**316**	G316DPA	

331	UPB331S	Leyland National 10351A/1R		B41F	1977	Ex London & Country, 1995
399	D101NDW	Leyland Lynx LX112TL11ZR1	Leyland	B49F	1987	Ex Maidstone & District, 1996
400	D102NDW	Leyland Lynx LX112TL11ZR1	Leyland	B49F	1987	Ex Maidstone & District, 1996
401	G34VME	Leyland Lynx LX2R11C15Z4S	Leyland	B49F	1989	Ex Kentish Bus, 1995
402	G35VME	Leyland Lynx LX2R11C15Z4S	Leyland	B49F	1989	Ex Kentish Bus, 1995
418	D156HML	Leyland Lynx LX112TL11ZR1	Leyland	B49F	1991	Ex Kentish Bus, 1996

430-437

		Mercedes-Benz 811D	Plaxton Beaver		B31F	1994	Ex London & Country, 1995

430	L430CPJ	**433**	L433CPJ	**435**	L435CPJ	**437**	L437CPJ
431	L431CPJ	**434**	L434CPJ	**436**	L436CPJ		

438	P438HKN	Mercedes-Benz 811D	Plaxton Beaver	B31F	1996	

440-453   Optare MetroRider MR17   Optare   B29F   1994   Ex London & Country, 1995

440	M440HPF	443	M443HPF	448	M448HPF	451	M451HPF
441	M441HPF	444	M444HPF	449	M449HPF	452	M452HPF
442	M442HPF	447	M447HPF	450	M450HPF	453	M453HPF

623-643   Volvo Citybus B10M-50   Northern Counties   H45/31F   1989   Ex London & Country, 1995

623	G623BPH	626	G626BPH	629	G629BPH	640	G640BPH	643	G643BPH
624	G624BPH	627	G627BPH	630	G630BPH	641	G641BPH		
625	G625BPH	628	G628BPH	639	G639BPH	642	G642BPH		

648-684   Volvo Citybus B10M-50   East Lancs   H45/31F   1990/91   Ex London & Country, 1995

648	H648GPF	656	H656GPF	664	H664GPF	673	H673GPF	681	H681GPF
649	H649GPF	657	H657GPF	665	H665GPF	674	H674GPF	682	H682GPF
650	H650GPF	658	H658GPF	667	H667GPF	675	H675GPF	683	H683GPF
651	H651GPF	659	H659GPF	668	H668GPF	676	H676GPF	684	H684GPF
652	H652GPF	660	H660GPF	669	H669GPF	677	H677GPF		
653	H653GPF	661	H661GPF	670	H670GPF	678	H678GPF		
654	H654GPF	662	H662GPF	671	H671GPF	679	H679GPF		
655	H655GPF	663	H663GPF	672	H672GPF	680	H680GPF		

685-700   Volvo Olympian YN2RC16Z4   East Lancs   H44/30F   1994   Ex London & Country, 1995

685	M685HPF	689	M689HPF	693	M693HPF	697	M697HPF
686	M686HPF	690	M690HPF	694	M694HPF	698	M698HPF
687	M687HPF	691	M691HPF	695	M695HPF	699	M699HPF
688	M688HPF	692	M692HPF	696	M696HPF	700	M700HPF

701	G640CHF	Volvo Citybus B10M-50	East Lancs	H49/39F	1989	Ex North Western, 1996
702	G641CHF	Volvo Citybus B10M-50	East Lancs	H49/39F	1989	Ex North Western, 1996
704	G643EKA	Volvo Citybus B10M-50	East Lancs	H49/39F	1990	Ex North Western, 1996
710	G661DTJ	Volvo Citybus B10M-50	East Lancs	H49/39F	1990	Ex North Western, 1996

721-733   Volvo Citybus B10M-50   Alexander RV   H47/29D   1989   Ex Kentish Bus, 1996

721	F101TML	724	F104TML	727	F107TML	730	F110TML	733	F113TML
722	F102TML	725	F105TML	728	F108TML	731	F111TML		
723	F103TML	726	F106TML	729	F109TML	732	F112TML		

845	E35NEF	MCW Metrorider MF154/9	Metro-Cammell-Weymann	DP31F	1988	Ex Darlington, 1995
846	E36NEF	MCW Metrorider MF154/9	Metro-Cammell-Weymann	DP31F	1988	Ex Darlington, 1995
847	E136KYW	MCW Metrorider MF150/38	Metro-Cammell-Weymann	B25F	1987	Ex Darlington, 1995
848	E140KYW	MCW Metrorider MF150/38	Metro-Cammell-Weymann	B25F	1987	Ex Darlington, 1995
849	E141KYW	MCW Metrorider MF150/38	Metro-Cammell-Weymann	B25F	1987	Ex Darlington, 1995
850	E145KYW	MCW Metrorider MF150/38	Metro-Cammell-Weymann	B25F	1987	Ex Darlington, 1995
851	E149KYW	MCW Metrorider MF150/38	Metro-Cammell-Weymann	B25F	1987	Ex Darlington, 1995
865	F865LCU	MCW Metrorider MF158/15	Metro-Cammell-Weymann	B31F	1988	Ex Kentish Bus, 1996

Previous Registrations

F106TML	F107TML
F107TML	F111TML
F109TML	F106TML
F110TML	F109TML
F111TML	F110TML

LONDON TRANSPORT BUSES

172 Buckingham Palace Road, London SW1W 9TN

The Procurement Directorate of London Transport Buses assumed responsibility for the tendering of services within Greater London on 1st April 1993 in succession to the Tendered Bus Division. The Procurement Directorate also acts in association with local authorities for certain specialised routes in Brent, Ealing, Hounslow, Kingston and Sutton, mostly for the disabled.

The negotiated net cost arrangements that have applied to previously untendered 'red bus' routes since 1993 will, by 2001, all be placed onto a formally-tendered basis. From April 1997, contracts will be issued on a Tendered Net Cost basis, under which the operator retains any revenue in excess of the price agreed with LT for the contract. Other ex-LBL routes meanwhile operate on a Tendered Gross Cost basis, where LT retain the revenue and the contract price is intended to cover the operator's costs.

For routes which pass into Greater London, particularly those of the former London Country operators, a 'fares and services' agreement is reached. Generally, the sections of these routes within London are operated under contract to LT, and are governed by LT fare scales and ticketing arrangements.

Other routes which enter or operate within the LT area without forming part of the LT system, such as some of the commercial routes worked by Metrobus, come under a London Bus Agreement under section 3 (2) of the LRT Act of 1984 for that part of the route which falls within the LT area.

As and when new contracts are issued for routes which pass into the central London area, a requirement is imposed that the vehicle livery should comprise at least 80% of traditional red. This requirement effectively outlaws the use of vehicles in allover advertising liveries (though full-rear advertisements are allowed). Such vehicles are therefore only to be found on contract services or dedicated driver-training duties. It also means that operators who have a separate livery scheme of their own, such as Capital Citybus and Stagecoach companies, can only use vehicles in this livery outside the central area.

Following the sale of the subsidiary operators in 1994/5, LTB came into possession of 83 vehicles on 4th March 1995. Of those, 30 RMs formed a reserve fleet, which was placed in store and maintained by Universitybus at Hatfield. These are all in traditional London red livery with white relief. In January 1997, two of these vehicles were sold to London United for increased service requirements, and two to MTL London for spares. The 26 remaining vehicles are listed below; it is probable that others will be dispersed shortly. There are also 46 RMLs leased to Sovereign London (formerly BTS, Borehamwood) and Kentish Bus, in the liveries of those operators, with whom they remain in stock as shown in the separate fleet listings.

LTB also own a low-floor Dennis Dart (DLP1) which is currently on extended evaluation by CentreWest, and a low-floor Volvo (VWL1) which is in extended use by London General. These are listed under those operators.

Purchased by London Transport for evaluation, DLP1 is currently in use by CentreWest from Westbourne Park garage. It is a low-floor version of the Plaxton-bodied Dennis Dart and an offside view of the bus while working from Uxbridge garage will be found on page 20. Here it is seen in Bishops Bridge Road. Capital Transport

LONDON TRANSPORT BUSES (Reserve fleet, all unlicensed)

RM32-2213   AEC Routemaster 5RM   Park Royal   H36/28R   1959-65

32	XYJ428	659	KFF239	1138	138CLT	1428	428CLT	2173	CUV173C
264	VLT264	736	XYJ418	1204	204CLT	1562	562CLT	2213	CUV213C
295	VLT295	966	WLT966	1205	XYJ429	1676	676DYE		
324	WLT324	995	WLT995	1214	214CLT	1825	825DYE		
342	KFF277	1005	ALC290A	1292	NVS485	2021	ALM21B		
385	WLT385	1078	KGH925A	1330	KGH975A	2050	ALM50B		

Previous registrations

ALC290A	5CLT	KGH925A	78CLT	XYJ418	WLT736
KFF239	WLT659	KGH975A	330CLT	XYJ428	VLT32
KFF277	WLT342	NVS485	292CLT	XYJ429	205CLT

LONDON UNITED/WESTLINK

London United Busways Ltd, Wellington Road, Fulwell, Middlesex, TW2 5NX
Stanwell Bus Co Ltd, 6 Pulborough Way, Hounslow, Middlesex, TW4 6DE

London United was purchased by a management-led team on 5th November 1994, taking 464 vehicles. These included 194 Dennis Darts, by far the largest gathering of the type in the former LBL fleet.

Following trials, traditional London livery of red with white relief has been developed. RMLs have grey relief and deep yellow transfers; Darts used for bus work have white roofs; some other vehicles have silver grey roof, grey upper-deck window-surrounds, and a thin white band below the upper-deck windows and above the grey skirt. Airbus vehicles are all-red with deep yellow lettering.

In addition to the usual ebb and flow of LT contracts, the Airbus operation has been revised and updated with 20 new Volvo Olympians carrying Alexander Royale bodywork. A new Airbus Direct service, furnished by 35 Dennis Darts, provides a contract booking link between the terminals of Heathrow Airport and hotels in central London.

In September 1995 the holding company of London United purchased Stanwell Buses. This company had been bought by a management-led team on 20th January 1994, taking 119 vehicles. Ownership of the fleet passed to the West Midlands Travel group on 24th March 1994; they, in turn, were purchased by the National Express group early in April 1995. Increasing rationalisation is now occurring between the fleets. Many LSs surplus to Westlink requirements have been rebuilt to Urban Bus specification and translated to London United. The distinctive Westlink livery of red with white and turquoise relief is now being amended to come more into line with London United styles.

The London United fleet operates from garages at Fulwell, Hounslow and Shepherds Bush. Airbus vehicles are based at West Ramp, Heathrow and maintained at Stamford Brook. The Westlink fleet operates from garages at Kingston and Hounslow Heath, although all major maintenance is undertaken at the latter site.

London United have introduced grey relief and yellow decals for their Routemasters, together with the new logo. RML2646 shows that London United were still using white-out-of-black blinds in July 1996, as well as demonstrating the opening cab window which is still useful in summer weather.
Stephen Madden

During the past year, the Airbus fleet of Metrobuses has been downgraded to ordinary bus operation. M1009, freshly-outshopped, was found at Kingston in July 1996 sporting the new fleet livery as it commenced its westbound trip to West Molesey. Geoff Rixon

The 1996 delivery of Volvo Olympians for Airbus services was followed by ten similar vehicles fitted out for normal bus service on newly-acquired contract route 131. VA7 was caught in Kingston in the early days of operation. Tony Wilson

The twenty-three Leyland Olympians delivered in 1991 with Leyland bodywork have recently been displaced from route 237, having been transferred to Hounslow garage. L312, one of three with high-back seating, was intercepted at Harlington Corner in September 1996. Colin Brown

The current generation of Airbus double deckers comprises 19 Volvo Olympians with Alexander Royale bodywork delivered in 1995/96. The vehicles do not carry their fleet numbers. No.A129 is seen at Baker Street in June 1996. Martin Ruthe

LONDON UNITED/WESTLINK

A112–130 Volvo Olympian YN2RV18Z4 Alexander Royale DPH43/9F 1995/96

112	N112UHP	117	N117UHP	122	N122UHP	127	N127YRW	
113	N113UHP	118	N118UHP	123	N123UHP	128	N128YRW	
114	N114UHP	119	N119UHP	124	N124YRW	129	N129YRW	
115	N115UHP	120	N120UHP	125	N125YRW	130	N130YRW	
116	N116UHP	121	N121UHP	126	N126YRW			

CD1–8 Dennis Dart SFD212BR1TGW1 Wright Crusader B32F 1996

1	VDZ8001	3	VDZ8003	5	VDZ8005	7	VDZ8007	
2	VDZ8002	4	VDZ8004	6	VDZ8006	8	VDZ8008	

DA1–9 DAF SB220LC550 Optare Delta B49F* 1989–90 * DA1 is DP49F
Ex London Buses, 1994
(DA1 ex Gailymatic, 1995)

1	F802NGY	3	G931MYG	5	G933MYG	7	G935MYG	9	G937MYG
2	A5LBR	4	G932MYG	6	G934MYG	8	G936MYG		

DR1–14 Dennis Dart 8.5SDL3003 Reeve Burgess Pointer B28F 1991 Ex London Buses, 1994

1	H101THE	5	H105THE	9	H109THE	13	H113THE	
2	H102THE	6	H106THE	10	H110THE	14	H114THE	
3	H103THE	7	H107THE	11	WLT931			
4	H104THE	8	H108THE	12	H112THE			

DR53–141 Dennis Dart 8.5SDL3010 Plaxton Pointer B24F* 1991–92 Ex London Buses, 1994
* DR53–57 are B28F

53	J653XHL	68	J368GKH	101	J101DUV	116	J116DUV	131	J131DUV
54	J654XHL	69	J369GKH	102	J102DUV	117	J117DUV	132	J132DUV
55	J655XHL	70	J370GKH	103	J103DUV	118	J118DUV	133	J133DUV
56	J156GAT	71	J371GKH	104	J104DUV	119	J119DUV	134	J134DUV
57	J157GAT	72	J372GKH	105	J105DUV	120	J120DUV	135	J135DUV
58	J158GAT	73	J373GKH	106	J106DUV	121	J121DUV	136	J136DUV
59	J159GAT	74	J374GKH	107	J107DUV	122	J122DUV	137	J137DUV
60	J160GAT	75	J375GKH	108	J108DUV	123	J123DUV	138	J138DUV
61	J161GAT	76	J376GKH	109	J109DUV	124	J124DUV	139	J139DUV
62	J362GKH	77	J377GKH	110	J110DUV	125	J125DUV	140	J140DUV
63	J363GKH	78	J378GKH	111	WLT946	126	J126DUV	141	J141DUV
64	J364GKH	79	J379GKH	112	J112DUV	127	J127DUV		
65	J365GKH	80	J380GKH	113	J113DUV	128	J128DUV		
66	J366GKH	99	J599DUV	114	J114DUV	129	J129DUV		
67	J367GKH	100	VLT23	115	J115DUV	130	J130DUV		

DRL96–108 Dennis Dart 9SDL3024 Plaxton Pointer B28F 1993 Ex London Buses, 1994

96	K96SAG	99	K199SAG	102	K102SAG	105	K105SAG	108	K108SAG
97	K97SAG	100	ALM2B	103	K103SAG	106	K106SAG		
98	K98SAG	101	K101SAG	104	K104SAG	107	K107SAG		

DRL159–171 Dennis Dart 9SDL3034 Plaxton Pointer B28F 1993 * DRL165–9 are B34F
Ex London Buses, 1994

159	L159XRH	162	L162XRH	165	L165YAT	168	L168YAT	171	L171CKH
160	L160XRH	163	L163XRH	166	L166YAT	169	L169YAT		
161	L161XRH	164	L164XRH	167	L167YAT	170	L170CKH		

DT1–27 Dennis Dart 8.5SDL3003 Duple Dartline DP21F 1990 Ex London Buses, 1994

1	G501VYE	7	G507VYE	13	G513VYE	19	G519VYE	25	G525VYE
2	G502VYE	8	G508VYE	14	G514VYE	20	G520VYE	26	G526VYE
3	G503VYE	9	G509VYE	15	G515VYE	21	G521VYE	27	G527VYE
4	G504VYE	10	G510VYE	16	G516VYE	22	G522VYE		
5	G505VYE	11	G511VYE	17	G517VYE	23	G523VYE		
6	G506VYE	12	G512VYE	18	G518VYE	24	G524VYE		

The latest single-deckers in the fleet are low-floor Dennis Darts with Wright bodywork. CD7 was caught at Hanworth Station in November 1996, freshly into service. Geoff Rixon

Six Leyland Lynxes are held at Hounslow. LX6 shows off the new livery to good effect at Hampton Court in August 1996 on route 111. Geoff Rixon

Westlink's fleet of Leyland Nationals began to receive the new livery at the end of 1996. LS7 is seen at Hampton in January 1997. Geoff Rixon

Thirteen of Westlink's Leyland Nationals have been refurbished as urban buses, including single-door conversion, and transferred to London United for use from Hounslow garage. LS268 runs through St Margaret's on the usual haunt of the type, route H37. Stephen Madden

DT29–167 Dennis Dart 8.5SDL3003 Carlyle Dartline B28F* 1990–91 * DT29, DT41/3–7 are DP21F; DT73/5/9 are B26F
Ex London Buses, 1994

29	G29TGW	51	G51TGW	76	H76MOB	144	H144MOB	155	H155MOB
41	G41TGW	52	G52TGW	77	WLT339	145	H145MOB	158	H158NON
42	G42TGW	53	G53TGW	78	H78MOB	146	H146MOB	159	H159NON
43	G43TGW	54	G54TGW	79	H79MOB	147	H147MOB	160	H160NON
44	G44TGW	56	G56TGW	80	236CLT	148	H148MOB	161	H161NON
45	G45TGW	57	G57TGW	81	H81MOB	149	H149MOB	162	H162NON
46	G46TGW	71	H71MOB	82	H82MOB	150	H150MOB	163	H163NON
47	G47TGW	72	H72MOB	83	H83MOB	151	H151MOB	164	WLT804
48	G48TGW	73	H73MOB	84	H84MOB	152	H152MOB	165	H165NON
49	G49TGW	74	H74MOB	85	H85MOB	153	H153MOB	166	H166NON
50	G50TGW	75	WLT329	86	H86MOB	154	H154MOB	167	H167NON

DT168 500CLT Dennis Dart 8.5SDL3003 Duple Dartline DP21F 1989 Ex London Buses, 1994

DWL1–14 Dennis Dart 9SDL3002 Wright Handybus B36F 1990 Ex London Buses, 1994

1	JDZ2401	4	JDZ2404	7	JDZ2407	10	JDZ2410	13	JDZ2413
2	JDZ2402	5	JDZ2405	8	JDZ2408	11	JDZ2411	14	JDZ2414
3	JDZ2403	6	JDZ2406	9	JDZ2409	12	JDZ2412		

FR1–8 Iveco Daily 49–10 Reeve Burgess Beaver B20FL 1990 Ex London Buses, 1994

1u	H701YUV	3u	H703YUV	5u	H705YUV	7u	H707YUV	
2u	H702YUV	4u	H704YUV	6u	H706YUV	8u	H708YUV	

FS29 C501HOE Ford Transit 190D Carlyle B20F 1985 Ex London Buses, 1994

L292–314 Leyland Olympian ONCL10/1RZ* Leyland H47/31F* 1989 * L306–14 are ON2R50C13Z4; L312–4 are DPH43/29F
Ex London Buses, 1994

292	G292UYT	297	G297UYT	302	G302UYT	307	G307UYT	312	G312UYT
293	G293UYT	298	G298UYT	303	G303UYT	308	G308UYT	313	G313UYT
294	G294UYT	299	G299UYT	304	G304UYT	309	G309UYT	314	G314UYT
295	G295UYT	300	G300UYT	305	G305UYT	310	G310UYT		
296	G296UYT	301	G301UYT	306	G306UYT	311	G311UYT		

LLW1–10 Dennis Lance SLF 11SDA3202 Wright Pathfinder 320 B34D 1993–94 Ex London Buses, 1994

1	ODZ8901	3	ODZ8903	5	ODZ8905	7	ODZ8907	9	ODZ8909
2	ODZ8902	4	ODZ8904	6	ODZ8906	8	ODZ8908	10	ODZ8910

Facing page **Earlier Darts are gradually receiving a revised livery incorporating mushroom roof with white lining-out. DR126 stands at East Acton; behind it can be seen another example of the class still in the original livery.** Colin Brown

Left **In 1995 Westlink received eight Optare-bodied MAN buses for use on route 371. MV8, originally numbered VA8, arrives at Kingston.** Tony Wilson

LS7	KJD507P	Leyland National 10351A/2R		DP33D	1976	Ex London Buses, 1994
LS13	KJD513P	Leyland National 10351A/2R		B36D	1976	Ex London Buses, 1994
LS24	KJD524P	Leyland National 10351A/2R		B36D	1976	Ex London Buses, 1994
LS29u	KJD529P	Leyland National 10351A/2R		B36D	1976	Ex London Buses, 1994
LS30	KJD530P	Leyland National 10351A/2R		DP42F	1976	Ex London Buses, 1994
LS35	KJD535P	Leyland National 10351A/2R		DP35D	1976	Ex London Buses, 1994
LS61	OJD861R	Leyland National 10351A/2R		B36D	1977	Ex London Buses, 1994
LS84	OJD884R	Leyland National 10351A/2R	(urban bus)	B38F	1977	Ex West Midlands, 1995
LS88	OJD888R	Leyland National 10351A/2R		DP36F	1977	Ex London Buses, 1994
LS96	OJD896R	Leyland National 10351A/2R		B38F	1977	Ex London Buses, 1994
LS97	OJD897R	Leyland National 10351A/2R		DP35D	1977	Ex London Buses, 1994
LS98	OJD898R	Leyland National 10351A/2R		B36D	1977	Ex London Buses, 1994
LS99	OJD899R	Leyland National 10351A/2R	(urban bus)	B38F	1977	Ex London Buses, 1994
LS112	THX112S	Leyland National 10351A/2R		B36F	1977	Ex London Buses, 1994
LS116u	THX116S	Leyland National 10351A/2R	(urban bus)	B38F	1977	Ex London Buses, 1994
LS123	THX123S	Leyland National 10351A/2R		DP40F	1977	Ex London Buses, 1994
LS150	THX150S	Leyland National 10351A/2R		B36D	1977	Ex London Buses, 1994
LS153	THX153S	Leyland National 10351A/2R	(urban bus)	B38F	1977	Ex West Midlands, 1995
LS195	THX195S	Leyland National 10351A/2R		B36D	1978	Ex London Buses, 1994
LS227	THX227S	Leyland National 10351A/2R		DP36DL	1978	Ex London Buses, 1994
LS245	THX245S	Leyland National 10351A/2R		DP40F	1978	Ex London Buses, 1994
LS251	THX251S	Leyland National 10351A/2R		B36D	1978	Ex London Buses, 1994
LS259	THX259S	Leyland National 10351A/2R		DP36D	1978	Ex London Buses, 1994
LS268	YYE268T	Leyland National 10351A/2R	(urban bus)	B38F	1978	Ex West Midlands, 1995
LS297	YYE297T	Leyland National 10351A/2R	(urban bus)	B38F	1979	Ex London Buses, 1994
LS304	AYR304T	Leyland National 10351A/2R		B363D	1979	Ex London Buses, 1994
LS335	AYR335T	Leyland National 10351A/2R	(urban bus)	B38F	1979	Ex London Buses, 1994
LS337	AYR337T	Leyland National 10351A/2R	(urban bus)	B38F	1979	Ex London Buses, 1995
LS363t	BYW363V	Leyland National 10351A/2R		B36D	1979	Ex London Buses, 1994
LS373	BYW373V	Leyland National 10351A/2R	(urban bus)	B38F	1979	Ex West Midlands, 1995
LS381t	BYW381V	Leyland National 10351A/2R		B36D	1979	Ex London Buses, 1994
LS385	BYW385V	Leyland National 10351A/2R	(urban bus)	B38F	1979	Ex London Buses, 1994
LS395	BYW395V	Leyland National 10351A/2R	(urban bus)	B38F	1979	Ex London Buses, 1994
LS405	BYW405V	Leyland National 10351A/2R	(urban bus)	B38F	1979	Ex West Midlands, 1995
LS408	BYW408V	Leyland National 10351A/2R		B36D	1979	Ex London Buses, 1994
LS411	BYW411V	Leyland National 10351A/2R		DP35D	1979	Ex London Buses, 1994
LS422	BYW422V	Leyland National 10351A/2R		B36D	1979	Ex London Buses, 1994
LS429	BYW429V	Leyland National 10351A/2R		B36D	1979	Ex West Midlands, 1995
LS431	BYW431V	Leyland National 10351A/2R	(urban bus)	B38F	1979	Ex London Buses, 1994
LS434	BYW434V	Leyland National 10351A/2R		B36D	1979	Ex London Buses, 1994

LX3–8		Leyland Lynx LX2R11C15Z4S	Leyland	B49F	1989	Ex London Buses, 1994

3	G73UYV	**5**	G75UYV	**7**	G77UYV	
4	G74UYV	**6**	G76UYV	**8**	G78UYV	

Top left **The last of the Dennis Darts with Plaxton bodywork delivered to London Buses before privatisation, DR171 carries dedicated livery for contract routes serving Heathrow. Here it is seen making short work of a mini-roundabout at Hatton Cross.** Malc McDonald

Centre left **Older Dennis Darts have been introduced on the new Airbus Direct services, which link Heathrow with major hotels in central London. DT2, at Hyde Park Corner in July 1996, shows the air-conditioning unit which was fitted as standard to the later conversions and is being retro-fitted to the earlier examples.** Stephen Madden

Left **Westlink's stretched Metroriders have started to appear in thie new livery. MRL91, with high-back seating, was found at West Molesey in August 1996.** Geoff Rixon

This page top **Fourteen Dennis Darts with Wright bodywork were delivered to Westlink in 1990, introducing the DWL class. DWL3 now carries dedicated livery for Kingston University.** Colin Lloyd

Above **Eight Iveco Daily vehicles with Reeve Burgess bodywork adapted to convey wheelchairs operated until the end of 1996 from Hounslow depot but are now delicensed. FR1 demonstrates the dedicated livery of the type at Hatton Cross in July 1996.** Colin Brown

M8–52

MCW Metrobus DR101/8   Metro-Cammell-Weymann   H43/28D*   1978–79   *Trainers are H0/15D
Ex London Buses, 1994

8	WYW8T	19	WYW19T	29	WYW29T	36t	WYW36T	46t	WYW46T
13t	WYW13T	21	WYW21T	30t	WYW30T	39	WYW39T	52	WYW52T
15	WYW15T	22t	WYW22T	31t	WYW31T	43	WYW43T		
17	WYW17T	28	WYW28T	34	WYW34T	44	WYW44T		

M59–204

MCW Metrobus DR101/9   Metro-Cammell-Weymann   H43/28D*   1979   *M147 is H0/15D
Ex London Buses, 1994

59	WYW59T	99	BYX99V	134	BYX134V	159	BYX159V	193	BYX193V
68	WYW68T	100	BYX100V	138	BYX138V	162	BYX162V	195	BYX195V
86	WYW86T	110	BYX110V	146	BYX146V	179	BYX179V	203	BYX203V
89	WYW89T	112	BYX112V	147t	BYX147V	183	BYX183V	204	BYX204V
93	WYW93T	122	BYX122V	154	BYX154V	186	BYX186V		
96	BYX96V	131	BYX131V	157	BYX157V	187	BYX187V		

M206–462

MCW Metrobus DR101/12   Metro-Cammell-Weymann   H43/28D*   1980   *M206/64 are H0/15D
Ex London Buses, 1994

206t	BYX206V	227	BYX227V	363	GYE363W	415	GYE415W
221	BYX221V	264t	BYX264V	366	GYE366W	462	GYE462W
223	BYX223V	327	EYE327V	387	GYE387W		

M506–697

MCW Metrobus DR101/14   Metro-Cammell-Weymann   H43/28D   1981   Ex London Buses, 1994

506	GYE506W	554	GYE554W	598	GYE598W	687	KYV687X
526	GYE526W	592	GYE592W	685	KYV685X	697	KYV697X

M813–951

MCW Metrobus DR101/16   Metro-Cammell-Weymann   H43/28D   1983   Ex London Buses, 1994

813	OJD813Y	835	OJD835Y	844	OJD844Y	889	OJD889Y	951	A951SUL
815	OJD815Y	836	OJD836Y	856	OJD856Y	906	A906SUL		
831	OJD831Y	839	OJD839Y	864	OJD864Y	920	A920SUL		
832	OJD832Y	841	OJD841Y	881	OJD881Y	932	A932SUL		

M958–1003

MCW Metrobus DR101/17   Metro-Cammell-Weymann   H43/28D   1984   *M1003 is DPH43/28D
Ex London Buses, 1994

958	A958SYF	966	A966SYF	980	A980SYF	994	A994SYF
960	A960SYF	967	A967SYF	981	A981SYF	999	A999SYF
962	A962SYF	969	A969SYF	985	A985SYF	1001	A701THV
963	A963SYF	972	A972SYF	990	A990SYF	1003	A703THV

M1006–1029

MCW Metrobus DR101/18   Metro-Cammell-Weymann   DPH41/28D 1984   Ex London Buses, 1994

1006	A706THV	1011	A711THV	1016	A716THV	1021	A721THV	1026	A726THV
1007	A707THV	1012	A712THV	1017	A717THV	1022	A722THV	1027	A727THV
1008	A708THV	1013	A713THV	1018	A718THV	1023	A723THV	1028	A728THV
1009	A709THV	1014	A714THV	1019	A719THV	1024	A724THV	1029	A729THV
1010	A710THV	1015	A715THV	1020	A720THV	1025	A725THV		

M1030–1439

MCW Metrobus DR101/17*   Metro-Cammell-Weymann   H43/28D* 1984–86 *M1048–53 are DR101/19;
M1251 is DPH43/28D Ex London Buses, 1994

1030	A730THV	1125	B125WUL	1200	B200WUL	1266	B266WUL	1352	C352BUV
1037	A737THV	1166	B166WUL	1207	B207WUL	1269	B269WUL	1353	C353BUV
1039	A739THV	1171	B171WUL	1212	B212WUL	1270	B270WUL	1356	C356BUV
1048	A748THV	1172	B172WUL	1238	B238WUL	1271	B271WUL	1358	C358BUV
1050	A750THV	1178	B178WUL	1240	B240WUL	1272	B272WUL	1360	C360BUV
1053	A753THV	1184	B184WUL	1242	B242WUL	1336	C336BUV	1361	C361BUV
1064	B64WUL	1187	B187WUL	1243	B243WUL	1341	C341BUV	1363	C363BUV
1069	B69WUL	1188	B188WUL	1251	B251WUL	1343	C343BUV	1368	C368BUV
1073	B73WUL	1190	B190WUL	1257	B257WUL	1344	C344BUV	1374	C374BUV
1106	B106WUL	1191	B191WUL	1261	B261WUL	1345	C345BUV	1381	C381BUV
1110	B110WUL	1194	B194WUL	1262	B262WUL	1351	C351BUV	1439	C439BUV

MR1–11

MCW Metrorider MF150/14   Metro-Cammell-Weymann   B23F   1987   Ex London Buses, 1994

1u	D461PON	3u	D463PON	5u	D465PON	7u	D467PON	11u	D471PON
2u	D462PON	4u	D464PON	6u	D466PON	10u	D470PON		

MR23–52   MCW Metrorider MF150/38   Metro-Cammell-Weymann   B25F   1987   Ex London Buses, 1994

23u	E123KYW	31u	E131KYW	39u	E139KYW	47u	E147KYW
30	E130KYW	34	E134KYW	42u	E142KYW	52u	E152KYW

MR134 D482NOX   MCW Metrorider MF150/2   Metro-Cammell-Weymann   B25F   1986   Ex London Buses, 1994

MRL78–92   MCW Metrorider MF158/11   Metro-Cammell-Weymann   B28F*   1988   * MRL89–92 are MF158/12 and DP31F; MRL78–80 are B19FL Ex London Buses, 1994

78	A2LBR	81	F185YDA	84	F188YDA	87	F191YDA	90	F194YDA
79	A3LBR	82	F186YDA	85	F189YDA	88	F192YDA	91	F195YDA
80	A4LBR	83	F187YDA	86	F190YDA	89	F193YDA	92	F196YDA

MRL108	F108YVP	MCW MetroRider MF150/16	Metro-Cammell-Weymann	B28F	1988	Ex London Buses, 1994
MRL115	F115YVP	MCW MetroRider MF150/16	Metro-Cammell-Weymann	B28F	1988	Ex London Buses, 1994
MRL116	F116YVP	MCW MetroRider MF150/16	Metro-Cammell-Weymann	B28F	1988	Ex London Buses, 1994
MRL117	F117YVP	MCW MetroRider MF150/16	Metro-Cammell-Weymann	B28F	1988	Ex London Buses, 1994

MV1–8   MAN 11.190   Optare Vecta   B42F   1995

1	N281DWY	3	N283DWY	5	N285DWY	7	N287DWY
2	N282DWY	4	N284DWY	6	N286DWY	8	N288DWY

RM2033	ALM33B	AEC Routemaster 5RM	Park Royal	H36/28R	1964	Ex LT Buses, 1994
RM2078	ALM78B	AEC Routemaster 5RM	Park Royal	H36/28R	1964	Ex LT Buses, 1994

RML880–2757   AEC Routemaster 7RM   Park Royal   H40/32R   1961–68   Ex London Buses, 1994; Cummins engines

880	WLT880	2432	JJD432D	2600	NML600E	2702	SMK702F	2744	SMK744F
881	WLT881	2447	JJD447D	2621	NML621E	2704	SMK704F	2751	SMK751F
891	WLT891	2455	JJD455D	2622	NML622E	2707	SMK707F	2757	SMK757F
2269	CUV269C	2463	JJD463D	2645	NML645E	2720	SMK720F		
2293	CUV293C	2464	JJD464D	2646	NML646E	2721	SMK721F		
2298	CUV298C	2485	JJD485D	2650	NML650E	2722	SMK722F		
2349	CUV349C	2489	JJD489D	2662	SMK662F	2729	SMK729F		
2353	CUV353C	2500	JJD500D	2697	SMK697F	2734	SMK734F		
2414	JJD414D	2519	JJD519D	2700	SMK700F	2739	SMK739F		

RML880 carries unofficial fleet number ER880

VA1–10   Volvo Olympian YN2RV18Z4   Alexander Royale   H45/29F   1996

Previous registrations

1	N131YRW	3	N133YRW	5	N135YRW	7	N137YRW	9	N139YRW
2	N132YRW	4	N134YRW	6	N136YRW	8	N138YRW	10	N140YRW

VT1t   YTA612S   Volvo B58–61   Duple Dominant II C53F   1977   Ex London Buses, 1994

A2LBR	F182YDA	VLT23	J610DUV	WLT946	J611DUV
A3LBR	F183YBA	WLT329	H575MOC	236CLT	H880LOX
A4LBR	F184YBA	WLT339	H577MOC	500CLT	G349GCK
ALM2B	K210SAG	WLT804	H264NON		
F802NGY	F54CWY, WLT400	WLT931	H611TKU		

Special liveries
Airbus livery: A112–30
Airbus Direct livery: DT1–27/9, DT41/3–7, DT168
London Borough of Hounslow livery: FR1–8
London United Tramways livery: M1069, RML880
Overall advertisements: LS112, LS227
Kingston University livery: DWL1–3, MR134

Disposition of fleet
London United: A112-30, CD1-8, DR1-9, DR60/5/6/8/70-117/23-41, DRL96-108/59-71, DT1-168, FR1-8, L292-314, LLW1-10, LS84, LS96/9, LS153, LS268/97, LS335/7/73/81/5/95, LS405/31, LX3-8, M8-1439, MRL109/15-7, RM2033/78, RML880-2757, VA1-10.
Stanwell Buses: DA1-9, DR10-4, DR53-9/61-4/7/9, DR118/22, DWL1-14, FS29, LS7, LS13, LS24, LS30/5, LS61, LS88, LS97/8, LS112/4/23/50/95, LS227/45/51/9, LS304/63, LS408/11/22/9/34, MR1-134, MRL78-92, MV1-8, VT1.

METROBUS

Metrobus Ltd, Oak Farm, Farnborough Hill, Orpington, Kent, BR6 6DA

Following the collapse of the Orpington & District Bus Company in February 1981, operations were taken over by the Cranleigh-based Tillingbourne Bus Company from 2nd March 1981. A new company was formed, that of Tillingbourne (Metropolitan) Ltd, to provide peak-hour services between Forestdale and Croydon. Forestdale is a large housing estate five miles from the nearest railway station, and had never been served by London Transport services. The new Company worked hard to restore public confidence and by the end of 1981 operated three successful routes: the 353 from Croydon to Orpington, the 355 linking Croydon to Forestdale and the 357 between Croydon via Forestdale to Orpington. All three became part of the LT network in 1985.

Following a management-led buy-out on 24th September 1983, Metrobus Ltd was born and has since gone from strength to strength. Having successfully gained routes 61 and 361 from August 1986, thirteen former London Fleetlines were acquired and subsequent gains saw the introduction of Leyland Lynxes and Olympians, Optare MetroRiders and Excels, Dennis Darts and, most recently, new Volvo Olympians.

LT routes operated are 138, 146, 161, 181, 261, 284, 693. Routes 351, 352, 353, 354, 356, 358, 361 are also operated with LT agreement. The fleet is in blue and yellow livery, and is kept at Oak Farm, Green Street Green.

A newcomer to the British bus scene is the Optare Excel low floor bus. One of the first operators in London to introduce this type was Metrobus of Orpington with ten vehicles allocated to route 358 between Crystal Palace and Orpington. Bromley High Street is the location in September 1996. Mike Harris

Seven Leyland Lynx buses are operated by Metrobus, six mark one types and a sole mark two example. Representing the former is D110NDW on route 354 at East Croydon in July 1996. Malc McDonald

Below A total of thirty-three Dennis Darts are now in service with Metrobus, proving just how popular this all-British vehicle has become during the last few years. K709KGU is seen on the Ramsden Estate in June while on route 353. Mike Harris

J813GGW is a Leyland Olympian with Leyland body new to Metrobus of Orpington in 1992. Route 353 is a peak hour Monday to Friday operation between Croydon and Orpington and is one of four double deck operated routes. Malc McDonald

Although Leyland Olympians and Dennis Darts make up the bulk of the Metrobus fleet, eight Optare MetroRiders are also owned. N904HWY is one of six bought new in 1996 for route 138. Stephen Madden

METROBUS

Bus Fleet

C395DML	Leyland Olympian ONLXB/1R	Eastern Coach Works	H43/34F	1985	
D103NDW	Leyland Lynx LX112TL11ZR1R	Leyland	B51F	1987	Ex Merthyr Tydfil, 1989
D104NDW	Leyland Lynx LX112TL11ZR1R	Leyland	B51F	1987	Ex Merthyr Tydfil, 1989
D110NDW	Leyland Lynx LX112TL11ZR1R	Leyland	B51F	1987	Ex Merthyr Tydfil, 1989
E575FTW	Ford Transit VE6	Ford	B11F	1988	Ex private owner, 1990
F80SMC	Leyland Lynx LX112L10ZR1	Leyland	DP49F	1988	
F165SMT	Leyland Lynx LX112L10ZR1	Leyland	B51F	1989	Ex Miller, Foxton, 1991
F166SMT	Leyland Lynx LX112L10ZR1	Leyland	B51F	1989	Ex Miller, Foxton, 1991
F802NGU	Leyland Olympian ONCL10/1RZ	Leyland	H47/31F	1989	
F803NGU	Leyland Olympian ONCL10/1RZ	Leyland	H47/31F	1989	

Leyland Olympian ON2R50C13Z4 — Leyland — H47/31F — 1990–92

G804SMV	H807XMY	H810AGX	J813GGW	K816HMV
G805SMV	H808AGX	H811AGX	K814HMV	
G806TMX	H809AGX	J812GGW	K815HMV	

Dennis Dart 8.5SDL3010 — Reeve Burgess Pointer — B32F* — 1991 — * J701EMX is DP32F

J701EMX	J703EMX	J705EMX	J707EMX
J702EMX	J704EMX	J706EMX	

Dennis Dart 9SDL3011 — Plaxton Pointer — B35F — 1992 — Ex Kentish Bus, 1996

J223HGY	J225HGY	J227HGY	J229HGY
J224HGY	J226HGY	J228HGY	

J968JNL	Optare MetroRider MR03	Optare	B25F	1991	Ex Kentish Bus, 1995
K101JMV	Leyland Lynx LX2R11C15Z4S	Leyland	B51F	1992	

Dennis Dart 9SDL3011 — Plaxton Pointer — B35F — 1992

K708KGU	K711KGU	K714KGU
K709KGU	K712KGU	K715KGU
K710KGU	K713KGU	K716KGU

L717OMV	Dennis Dart 9.8SDL3032	Plaxton Pointer	B35F	1994
L718OMV	Dennis Dart 9.8SDL3032	Plaxton Pointer	B35F	1994
L719OMV	Dennis Dart 9.8SDL3032	Plaxton Pointer	B35F	1994
L720OMV	Dennis Dart 9.8SDL3032	Plaxton Pointer	B35F	1994
M721CGO	Dennis Dart 9.8SDL3054	Plaxton Pointer	B35F	1994
M722CGO	Dennis Dart 9.8SDL3054	Plaxton Pointer	B35F	1995
M723CGO	Dennis Dart 9.8SDL3054	Plaxton Pointer	B35F	1995
M724CGO	Dennis Dart 9.8SDL3054	Plaxton Pointer	B35F	1995
N725KGF	Dennis Dart 9.8SDL3054	Plaxton Pointer	B35F	1995
N726KGF	Dennis Dart 9.8SDL3054	Plaxton Pointer	B35F	1995

Optare MetroRider MR17 — Optare — B26F — 1996

N901HWY	N903HWY	N905HWY
N902HWY	N904HWY	N906HWY

Optare L1070 — Optare Excel — B35F — 1996

P501OUG	P503OUG	P505OUG	P507OUG	P509OUG
P502OUG	P504OUG	P506OUG	P508OUG	P510OUG

Volvo Olympian — Northern Counties Palatine 1 — H47/29F — 1996

P817SGP	P821SGP	P824SGP	P828SGP
P818SGP	P822SGP	P825SGP	P829SGP
P819SGP	P823SGP	P826SGP	

The coach fleet is listed in the London Coach Handbook.

METROLINE

Metroline Travel Ltd, 118–122 College Road, Harrow, Middlesex, HA1 1DB

Metroline was purchased by a management-led team on 7th October 1994, taking 386 vehicles. On 28th November 1994, Atlas Bus was purchased by Metroline from the Pullmans Group, together with 26 Leyland Titans.

After a period of experiments, red livery with white relief has been augmented by a dark blue skirt. The separate Atlas Bus operation was wound up in August 1996, its Harlesden base having already been vacated operationally in January 1996.

The holding company of Metroline has also purchased the coach fleet of Brent's of Watford. Details of that fleet, which operates independently within the group, are included in the London Coach Handbook.

The fleet operates from garages at Cricklewood, Edgware, Harrow Weald, North Wembley and Willesden. Major maintenance of those based at North Wembley and of single-deckers from Edgware is undertaken at Harrow Weald; double-deckers from Edgware are maintained at Cricklewood. Vehicles are also allocated to the Contract Services (formerly Commercial Services) fleet, based at various garages as required.

Twenty-two Alexander bodied Olympians were received by Metroline in 1996, principally for route 52. AV13 is seen on a Christmas Day variation of the route at Trafalgar Square.
Paul Anderson

Metroline's low-floor Dennis Lances with Wright bodywork have now received updated livery. LLW26 presents a somewhat colourful presence at Golders Green in June 1996.
Herbee Thomas

Above **All of the Northern Counties-bodied Dennis Lances are currently based at Cricklewood garage. LN21, freshly-painted into new livery, pauses at Brent Cross in August 1996.**
Colin Brown

Centre **Some of Metroline's earlier Darts with Carlyle bodywork have now been placed in store. DT129, at Golders Green, and lacking side fleetname transfers, is one of those which remains in service.**
Colin Lloyd

Left **Metroline have a large consignment of Dennis Darts. DR90, at Golders Green in March 1996, represents those bodied by Plaxton.**
Colin Brown

Many of Metroline's Leyland Titans are now awaiting disposal, but some have found their way to the contract services fleet. As such, T459 was on loan to Willesden garage when photographed in Victoria in August 1996, working alongside others of the type on route 52, which has now been converted to newer vehicles. Colin Lloyd

METROLINE

AV1–22   Volvo Olympian   Alexander RH   H43/25D   1996

1	585CLT	6	P486MBY	11	P491MBY	16	P476MBY	21	P474MBY
2	P482MBY	7	P487MBY	12	P492MBY	17	P477MBY	22	P475MBY
3	P483MBY	8	P488MBY	13	P493MBY	18	P478MBY		
4	P484MBY	9	P489MBY	14	P494MBY	19	P479MBY		
5	P485MBY	10	P490MBY	15	P495MBY	20	P480MBY		

DR15–42   Dennis Dart 8.5SDL3003   Reeve Burgess Pointer   B28F*   1991   * DR40/2 are Plaxton Pointer B28F Ex London Buses, 1994

15	H115THE	17	H117THE	19	H119THE	42	H542XGK
16	H116THE	18	H118THE	40	H540XGK		

DR81–148   Dennis Dart 8.5SDL3010   Plaxton Pointer   B28F   1992   Ex London Buses, 1994

81	J381GKH	86	J386GKH	91	J391GKH	96	J396GKH	144	K244PAG
82	J382GKH	87	J387GKH	92	J392GKH	97	J397GKH	145	K245PAG
83	J383GKH	88	J388GKH	93	J393GKH	98	J398GKH	146	K246PAG
84	J384GKH	89	J389GKH	94	J394GKH	142	K242PAG	147	K247PAG
85	J385GKH	90	J390GKH	95	J395GKH	143	K243PAG	148	K248PAG

DT88–157   Dennis Dart 8.5SDL3003   Carlyle Dartline   B28F   1990–91   Ex London Buses, 1994

88	H588MOC	104u	H104MOB	115	H115MOB	126	H126MOB	137	H137MOB
89	H89MOB	105	H105MOB	116	H116MOB	127	H127MOB	138	H138MOB
90	H890LOX	106	H106MOB	117	H117MOB	128	H128MOB	139	H139MOB
92	H92MOB	107	H107MOB	118	H118MOB	129	H129MOB	140	H140MOB
93	H93MOB	108	H108MOB	119	H119MOB	130	H130MOB	141	H141MOB
94	H94MOB	109	H109MOB	120	H120MOB	131	H131MOB	142	H142MOB
98u	H98MOB	110	H110MOB	121	H621MOM	132	H132MOB	143	H143MOB
100	H620MOM	111	H611MOM	122	H122MOB	133	H133MOB	156	H156MOB
101u	H101MOB	112	H112MOB	123	H123MOB	134	H134MOB	157	H157NON
102	H102MOB	113	H113MOB	124	H124MOB	135	H135MOB		
103	H103MOB	114	H114MOB	125	H125MOB	136	H136MOB		

DTs 100 and 105 are on loan to Universitybus, Hatfield

EDR1–9
Dennis Dart 9.8SDL3040　　Plaxton Pointer　　B39F　　1994

1	M101BLE	3	M103BLE	5	M105BLE	7	M107BLE	9	M109BLE
2	M102BLE	4	M104BLE	6	M106BLE	8	M108BLE		

EDR10–44
Dennis Dart SFD412BR5TGD1　　Plaxton Pointer　　B39F　　1996

10	P285MLD	17	P292MLD	24	P299MLD	31	P307MLD	38	P314MLD
11	P286MLD	18	P293MLD	25	P301MLD	32	P308MLD	39	P315MLD
12	P287MLD	19	P294MLD	26	P302MLD	33	P309MLD	40	P316MLD
13	P288MLD	20	P295MLD	27	P303MLD	34	P310MLD	41	P317MLD
14	P289MLD	21	P296MLD	28	P304MLD	35	P311MLD	42	P318MLD
15	P290MLD	22	P297MLD	29	P305MLD	36	P312MLD	43	P319MLD
16	P291MLD	23	P298MLD	30	P306MLD	37	P313MLD	44	P320MLD

LLW25–38
Dennis Lance SLF 11SDA3202　　Wright Pathfinder 320　　B34D　　1993–94　　Ex London Buses, 1994

25	L25WLH	28	L28WLH	31	L31WLH	34	L34WLH	37	L37WLH
26	L26WLH	29	L29WLH	32	L32WLH	35	L35WLH	38	L38WLH
27	L27WLH	30	L21WLH	33	L39WLH	36	L36WLH		

LN1–31
Dennis Lance 11SDA3108　　Northern Counties Paladin　　B37D　　1993　　Ex London Buses, 1994

1	K301YJA	8	K308YJA	15	K315YJA	22	K322YJA	29	K329YJA
2	K302YJA	9	K309YJA	16	K316YJA	23	K323YJA	30	K330YJA
3	K303YJA	10	K310YJA	17	K317YJA	24	K324YJA	31	K331YJA
4	K304YJA	11	K311YJA	18	K318YJA	25	K325YJA		
5	K305YJA	12	K312YJA	19	K319YJA	26	K326YJA		
6	K306YJA	13	K313YJA	20	K320YJA	27	K327YJA		
7	K307YJA	14	K315YJA	21	K321YJA	28	K328YJA		

M1–5
MCW Metrobus DR101/3　　Metro-Cammell-Weymann　　H43/28F　　1978　　Ex London Buses, 1994

1	THX101S	2t	THX102S	3t	THX103S	4t	THX104S	5t	THX105S

M18	WYW18T	MCW Metrobus DR101/8	Metro-Cammell-Weymann	H43/28D	1979 Ex London Buses, 1994
M20	WYW20T	MCW Metrobus DR101/8	Metro-Cammell-Weymann	H43/28D	1979 Ex London Buses, 1994
M41	WYW41T	MCW Metrobus DR101/8	Metro-Cammell-Weymann	H43/28D	1979 Ex London Buses, 1994
M48	WYW48T	MCW Metrobus DR101/8	Metro-Cammell-Weymann	H43/28D	1979 Ex London Buses, 1994
M54	WYW54T	MCW Metrobus DR101/8	Metro-Cammell-Weymann	H43/28D	1979 Ex London Buses, 1994

M57–184
MCW Metrobus DR101/9　　Metro-Cammell-Weymann　　H43/28D　　1979　　Ex London Buses, 1994
(M135/7/50/92 ex Atlas Bus, 1996)

57	WYW57T	87	WYW87T	111t	BYX111V	140	BYX140V	172	BYX172V
58	WYW58T	88	WYW88T	113	BYX113V	142	BYX142V	178	BYX178V
62	WYW62T	90	WYW90T	119	BYX119V	150	BYX150V	180	BYX180V
70	WYW70T	91	WYW91T	125	BYX125V	151	BYX151V	184	BYX184V
73	WYW73T	94	WYW94T	127	BYX127V	155	BYX155V	192	BYX192V
77	WYW77T	97	BYX97V	128	BYX128V	163	BYX163V		
83	WYW83T	102	BYX102V	135	BYX135V	166	BYX166V		
84	WYW84T	107	BYX107V	136	BYX136V	167	BYX167V		
85	WYW85T	109	BYX109V	137	BYX137V	169	BYX169V		

M222–482
MCW Metrobus DR101/12　　Metro-Cammell-Weymann　　H43/28D　　1980　　Ex London Buses, 1994
(M222/324/52/73 ex London General, 1995; M272/6, M407 ex Atlas Bus, 1996)

222	BYX222V	326	EYE326V	394	GYE394W	438	GYE438W	460	GYE460W
238	BYX238V	335	EYE335V	403	GYE403W	440	GYE440W	461	GYE461W
272	BYX272V	342	EYE342V	407	GYE407W	443	GYE443W	467	GYE467W
276	BYX276V	344	EYE344V	409t	GYE409W	444	GYE444W	468	GYE468W
300	BYX300V	352	GYE352W	424	GYE424W	446t	GYE446W	473	GYE473W
306	BYX306V	367t	GYE367W	428	GYE428W	448	GYE448W	482	GYE482W
309	BYX309V	373	GYE373W	429	GYE429W	449	GYE449W		
313	BYX313V	376	GYE376W	432	GYE432W	453	GYE453W		
315	BYX315V	380	GYE380W	436	GYE436W	455	GYE455W		
324	EYE324V	391	GYE391W	437	GYE437W	459	GYE459W		

M524–696
MCW Metrobus DR101/14　　Metro-Cammell-Weymann　　H43/28D　　1981　　Ex London Buses, 1994

524	GYE524W	595	GYE595W	621	KYO621X	683	KYV683X
550	GYE550W	618	KYO618X	655	KYV655X	696	KYV696X

Metroline have settled on this variation of their livery for the RML fleet, used on routes 6 and 98. RML2547 is seen at Oxford Circus in June 1996. Geoff Rixon

Metroline have taken forty-four Dennis Darts into stock since privatisation, enabling replacement of older minibuses. EDR14 is one of the 1996 arrivals, seen at Harrow Weald on route H12. All of these vehicles are bodied by Plaxton. Capital Transport

Metroline's RM644 was converted to open-top in 1993, and appears occasionally on service as well as private hire work. In July 1996 it was found at Brent Cross on Tesco services. The platform door can just be made out in this photograph. Colin Brown

The first five Metrobuses to enter London service are now in the contract services fleet of Metroline. M1, lacking fleetnames and carrying non-standard livery, was caught at Brent Cross in July 1996. Colin Brown

M810–955 MCW Metrobus DR101/16 — Metro-Cammell-Weymann — H43/28D — 1983 — Ex London Buses, 1994

810	OJD810Y	910	A910SUL	924	A924SUL	937	A937SUL	950	A950SUL
819t	WLT342	911	A911SUL	935	A935SUL	945	A945SUL	955	A955SUL

M956–1431 MCW Metrobus DR101/17* — Metro-Cammell-Weymann — H43/28D* — 1984–86 — * M1047 is DR101/19; M1185/236 are DPH43/28D — Ex London Buses, 1994

956	A956SYF	1056	B56WUL	1192	B192WUL	1274	B274WUL	1423	C423BUV
968	A968SYF	1057	B57WUL	1193	B193WUL	1339	C339BUV	1425	C425BUV
974	A974SYF	1068	B68WUL	1195	B195WUL	1342	C342BUV	1426	C426BUV
982	A982SYF	1071	B71WUL	1197	B197WUL	1346	C346BUV	1427	C427BUV
993	A993SYF	1167	B167WUL	1198	B198WUL	1348	C348BUV	1428	C428BUV
995	A995SYF	1168	B168WUL	1202	B202WUL	1349	C349BUV	1429	WLT826
1004	A704THV	1174	B174WUL	1204	B204WUL	1350	C350BUV	1430	C430BUV
1031	A731THV	1181	B181WUL	1205	B205WUL	1366	C366BUV	1431	C431BUV
1034	A734THV	1183	B183WUL	1208	B208WUL	1383	C383BUV		
1035	A735THV	1185	WLT893	1218	B218WUL	1408	C408BUV		
1043	A743THV	1186	B186WUL	1236	WLT646	1409	C409BUV		
1047	A747THV	1189	B189WUL	1273	WLT902	1416	C416BUV		

RM70t	VLT70	AEC Routemaster 5RM	Park Royal	H36/28R	1959	Ex London Buses, 1994
RM644	WLT644	AEC Routemaster 5RM	Park Royal	O36/28RD	1961	Ex London Buses, 1994
RMC1513	513CLT	AEC Routemaster 6RM	Park Royal	H32/25RD	1962	Ex London Buses, 1994

RML893–2755 AEC Routemaster 7RM — Park Royal — H40/32R — 1961–68 — Ex London Buses, 1994; Cummins engines

893	KFF276	2368	JJD368D	2532	JJD532D	2651	NML651E	2713	SMK713F
902	ALC464A	2377	JJD377D	2537	JJD537D	2652	NML652E	2727	SMK727F
2274	CUV274C	2384	JJD384D	2547	JJD547D	2681	SMK681F	2728	SMK728F
2285	CUV285C	2430	JJD430D	2558	JJD558D	2689	SMK689F	2737	SMK737F
2288	CUV288C	2431	JJD431D	2566	JJD566D	2690	SMK690F	2755	SMK755F
2289	CUV289C	2439	JJD439D	2579	JJD579D	2695	SMK695F		
2299	CUV299C	2446	JJD446D	2585	JJD585D	2698	SMK698F		
2308	CUV308C	2471	JJD471D	2594	JJD594D	2701	SMK701F		
2312	CUV312C	2478	JJD478D	2599	NML599E	2703	SMK703F		
2331	CUV331C	2508	JJD508D	2634	NML634E	2706	SMK706F		
2348	CUV348C	2509	JJD509D	2649	NML649E	2710	SMK710F		

T287–518 Leyland Titan TNLXB2RR — Leyland — H44/24D* — 1981–82 — * T287, T319/21 are H44/26D — Ex Atlas Bus, 1996

287	KYN287X	343	KYV343X	415	KYV415X	459	KYV459X	482	KYV482X
302	KYN302X	357	KYV357X	419	KYV419X	475	KYV475X	485	KYV485X
313	KYV313X	375	KYV375X	432	KYV432X	477	KYV477X	518	KYV518X
319	KYV319X	388	KYV388X	433	KYV433X	478	KYV478X		
321	KYV321X	390	KYV390X	435	KYV435X	479	KYV479X		
341	KYV341X	399	KYV399X	438	KYV438X	481	KYV481X		

Previous registrations

ALC464A	WLT902	WLT342	OJD819Y	WLT826	C429BUV	WLT902	B273WUL
KFF276	WLT893	WLT646	B236WUL	WLT893	B185WUL	585CLT	P481MBY

Named vehicles
LN1 *Princess Madden*, RMC1513 *Queen Victoria*

Special liveries
Tesco livery : DT103
Safeway livery : DT88
Overall advertisement : M409

MTL LONDON

MTL London Northern Ltd, 17–19 Highgate Hill, London N19 5NA

London Northern was purchased by MTL Trust Holdings on 26th October 1994, taking 341 vehicles. The operations of London Suburban Bus, already owned by MTL, were absorbed on a staged basis up to June 1996. R&I Tours and their LT contracts were taken over in October 1995, and absorbed into the MTL London fleet in June 1996.

From December 1994 vehicles have appeared in unrelieved red livery. The coaching fleet was renewed in March 1995, introducing the SightseerS identity already used elsewhere in the MTL group, and this has since been adopted for coaches acquired from R&I Tours.

The fleet operates from garages at Holloway, North Acton and Potters Bar. Traffic area boundaries mean that vehicles based at Potters Bar are licensed in the Eastern traffic area. Holloway garage has the largest daily vehicle turn-out of any London garage.

Sixteen Volvo Olympians with Northern Counties bodywork were purchased by London Suburban Buses in 1993/4 and absorbed by MTL London in 1995. The clean livery makes an imposing sight of No.212 in August 1996. Stephen Madden

Amongst the latest single deckers in the MTL London fleet are eight Marshall bodied MAN buses ordered for route 79, won on tender in 1996. MM271 is seen at Canons Park.

MTL London have recently treated their standard Routemasters to a cosmetic repaint, in the course of which the cantrail relief has been lost. RM1171, well into its fourth decade of service, crosses Trafalgar Square in July 1996 on route 139, the normal haunt of the type. Stephen Madden

Nine Leyland Titans remain in service of those acquired from London Suburban when that operation was absorbed in 1995, though their days are now numbered. T111 starts its northbound journey at Waterloo in June 1996. Laurie Rufus

One of a kind in the MTL London fleet is this Marshall midibus allocated exclusively to the PB1. Russell Upcraft

Unique in the fleet is No.539, an Ikarus-bodied DAF single-decker new in 1991 and acquired after brief use by R&I. Seen in Hertford, with the route suffix displayed on the destination blind, this is one of three DAF single-deck buses in the fleet. Tony Wilson

MTL LONDON

DC216–229   Dennis Dart 9SDL3002   Duple/Carlyle   B36F   1990   Ex R&I, 1996

| 216 | G216LGK | 220 | G220LGK | 224 | G124RGT |
| 219 | G219LGK | 221 | G121RGT | 229 | G129RGT |

| DC232 | RIB7002 | Dennis Dart 9SDL3002 | Carlyle C26 | B36F | 1990 | Ex R&I, 1996 |
| DM242 | RIB8341 | Dennis Dart 9.8SDL3035 | Marshall C37 | B40F | 1994 | Ex R&I, 1996 |

DNL101–120   Dennis Dart 9SDL3034   Northern Counties Paladin   B34F   1994   Ex London Buses, 1994

101	L101HHV	105	L105HHV	109	L109HHV	114	L114HHV	118	L118HHV
102	L102HHV	106	L106HHV	110	L110HHV	115	L115HHV	119	L119HHV
103	L103HHV	107	L107HHV	112	L112HHV	116	L116HHV	120	L120HHV
104	L104HHV	108	L108HHV	113	L113HHV	117	L117HHV		

| DP233 | 33LUG | Dennis Dart 9.8SDL3017 | Plaxton Pointer | B40F | 1992 | Ex R&I, 1996 |

DP234–239   Dennis Dart 9SDL3011   Plaxton Pointer   B35F   1993   Ex R&I, 1996

| 234 | K414MGN | 236 | K416MGN | 238 | K418MGN |
| 235 | RIB5085 | 237 | K417MGN | 239 | K419MGN |

DP240	M498ALP	Dennis Dart 9SDL3031	Plaxton Pointer	B35F	1994	Ex R&I, 1996
DP241	M499ALP	Dennis Dart 9SDL3031	Plaxton Pointer	B35F	1994	Ex R&I, 1996
DP245	M503ALP	Dennis Dart 9.8SDL3054	Plaxton Pointer	B35F	1995	Ex R&I, 1996
DP246	M504ALP	Dennis Dart 9.8SDL3054	Plaxton Pointer	B35F	1995	Ex R&I, 1996
DP247	M505ALP	Dennis Dart 9.8SDL3054	Plaxton Pointer	B35F	1995	Ex R&I, 1996
DP248	M506ALP	Dennis Dart 9.8SDL3054	Plaxton Pointer	B35F	1995	Ex R&I, 1996

DRL18–37   Dennis Dart 9SDL3016   Plaxton Pointer   B34F+16   1992   Ex London Buses, 1994
                                                                                    (DRL30/5/6 ex R&I, 1996)

18	K818NKH	22	K822NKH	26	K826NKH	30	K430OKH	34	K434OKH
19	K819NKH	23	K823NKH	27	K827NKH	31	K431OKH	35	K435OKH
20	K820NKH	24	K824NKH	28	K828NKH	32	K432OKH	36	K436OKH
21	K821NKH	25	K825NKH	29	K429OKH	33	K433OKH	37	K437OKH

DT87–99   Dennis Dart 8.5SDL3003   Carlyle Dartline   B28F   1990   Ex Metroline, 1996

| DT87 | H87MOB | DT95 | H95MOB | DT97 | H97MOB |
| DT91 | H91MOB | DT96 | H96MOB | DT99 | H899LOX |

IC343	N713FLN	Iveco TurboDaily 59.12	Cacciamali Ibis	C20F	1995	Ex R&I, 1996
IC344	N714FLN	Iveco TurboDaily 59.12	Cacciamali Ibis	C20F	1995	Ex R&I, 1996
IR91	RIB8432	Iveco Daily 49.10	Robin Hood City Nippy	C12F	1989	Ex R&I, 1996

Dennis Darts were popular with R&I Tours as well as with London Northern. DP235, bodied by Plaxton, was new to R&I in 1993, subsequently gaining a cherished registration. In September 1996 it was found at Kensal Rise on route 46, which had been ceded to R&I by London Northern at retendering. Colin Brown

IR202	RIB5082	Iveco Daily 49.10	Robin Hood City Nippy	B23F	1989	Ex R&I, 1996	
IR203	RIB5083	Iveco Daily 49.10	Robin Hood City Nippy	B23F	1989	Ex R&I, 1996	
IR206	RIB4316	Iveco Daily 49.10	Robin Hood City Nippy	B15F	1989	Ex R&I, 1996	
IR207	RIB7003	Iveco Daily 49.10	Robin Hood City Nippy	B23F	1989	Ex R&I, 1996	
IR208	RIB7004	Iveco Daily 49.10	LHE	B23F	1989	Ex R&I, 1996	
IR210	G122CLD	Iveco Daily 49.10	Robin Hood	B19F	1989	Ex R&I, 1996	
IR348	N698FLN	Iveco Daily 49.10	Robin Hood	C12F	1995	Ex R&I, 1996	
LP342	RIB4315	LAG Panoramic	LAG	C32FT	1989	Ex R&I, 1996	

M9–199   MCW Metrobus DR101/9*   Metro-Cammell-Weymann   H43/28D   1978–79
*M9–42 are DR101/8
Ex London Buses, 1994
(M16, M37, M106/8 ex Merseybus, 1995; M117/39 ex London Suburban, 1995)

9	WYW9T	42	WYW42T	92	WYW92T	117	BYX117V	160	BYX160V
12	WYW12T	67	WYW67T	95	WYW95T	118	BYX118V	161	BYX161V
16	WYW16T	72	WYW72T	98	BYX98V	124	BYX124V	181	BYX181V
25	WYW25T	75	WYW75T	101	BYX101V	126	BYX126V	189	BYX189V
27	WYW27T	78	WYW78T	103	BYX103V	130	BYX130V	194	BYX194V
32	WYW32T	79	WYW79T	106	BYX106V	133	BYX133V	199	BYX199V
33	WYW33T	80	WYW80T	108	BYX108V	139	BYX139V		
35	WYW35T	81	WYW81T	114	BYX114V	145	BYX145V		
37	WYW37T	82	WYW82T	115	BYX115V	148	BYX148V		

M213–501   MCW Metrobus DR101/12   Metro-Cammell-Weymann   H43/28D   1980   Ex London Buses, 1994
(M229 ex London Suburban, 1995; M377, M501 ex Merseybus, 1995)

213	BYX213V	294	BYX294V	341	EYE341V	481	GYE481W
229	BYX229V	322	EYE322V	356	GYE356W	501	GYE501W
243	BYX243V	328	EYE328V	377	GYE377W		

M512–802   MCW Metrobus DR101/14   Metro-Cammell-Weymann   H43/28D   1981–82   Ex London Buses, 1994

512	GYE512W	571	GYE571W	594	GYE594W	656	KYV656X	764	KYV764X
560	GYE560W	572	GYE572W	608	KYO608X	674	KYV674X	797	KYV797X
561	GYE561W	574	GYE574W	616	KYO616X	677	KYV677X	800	KYV800X
563	GYE563W	576	GYE576W	620	KYO620X	678	KYV678X	801	KYV801X
564	GYE564W	578	GYE578W	623	KYO623X	693	KYV693X	802	KYV802X
565	GYE565W	579	GYE579W	639	KYV639X	739	KYV739X		
570	GYE570W	588	GYE588W	640	KYV640X	755	KYV755X		

M824–934   MCW Metrobus DR101/16   Metro-Cammell-Weymann   H43/28D   1983   Ex London Buses, 1994

824	OJD824Y	879	OJD879Y	912	A912SUL	921	A921SUL
829	OJD829Y	890	OJD890Y	915	A915SUL	925	A925SUL
876	OJD876Y	896	A896SUL	916	A916SUL	928	A928SUL
878	OJD878Y	899	A899SUL	917	A917SUL	934	A934SUL

Amongst vehicles acquired from R&I Tours in 1996 were five Optare-bodied MAN single-deckers. MV250 leaves Brent Cross in August 1996 on its way around the North Circular Road to Ealing. Colin Brown

Shortly before privatisation, nineteen Dennis Darts with Northern Counties bodywork joined what was then the London Northern fleet for contract route C2. DNL101 shows the Camden Link livery adopted for many of the batch in Regent Street in June 1996. Geoff Rixon

Fifteen further MAN chassis were bodied by Marshall to form what has now become the MM class when R&I gained the contract for route 95. MM257 joins the main road at Dormers Wells in April 1996. Mike Harris

The former London Northern company received the entire 1993 delivery of twenty Mercedes-Benz midibuses with Wright bodywork. MW37, the last of the batch, surrendered its original Irish registration to a coach which has since been sold. This view was taken at Turnpike Lane in September 1996. Mike Harris

M957–1414   MCW Metrobus DR101/17   Metro-Cammell-Weymann   H43/28D*   1984–86 * M1045/52 are DR101/19;
M1045 is DPH43/28D; M1080 is H43/30F; M1393/6 are DPH38/28F
Ex London Buses, 1994

957	A957SYF	1060	B60WUL	1114	B114WUL	1156	B156WUL	1333	C333BUV
961t	A961SYF	1061	B61WUL	1115	B115WUL	1157	B157WUL	1334	C334BUV
964	A964SYF	1063	B63WUL	1117	B117WUL	1158	B158WUL	1355	C355BUV
971	A971SYF	1065	B65WUL	1118	B118WUL	1159	B159WUL	1365	C365BUV
987	A987SYF	1066	B66WUL	1119	B119WUL	1160	B160WUL	1369	C369BUV
989	A989SYF	1067t	B67WUL	1120	B120WUL	1161	B161WUL	1385	C385BUV
997	A997SYF	1072	B72WUL	1141	B141WUL	1163	B163WUL	1390	C390BUV
1032	A732THV	1076	B76WUL	1142	B142WUL	1234	B234WUL	1392	C392BUV
1033	A733THV	1077	B77WUL	1143	B143WUL	1250	B250WUL	1393	C393BUV
1038	A738THV	1078	B78WUL	1145	B145WUL	1277	B277WUL	1394	C394BUV
1040	A740THV	1079	B79WUL	1146	B146WUL	1284	B284WUL	1395	C395BUV
1041	A741THV	1080t	B80WUL	1147	B147WUL	1287	B287WUL	1396	C396BUV
1042	A742THV	1081	B81WUL	1148	B148WUL	1292	B292WUL	1397	C397BUV
1045t	A745THV	1082	B82WUL	1149	B149WUL	1325	C325BUV	1403	C403BUV
1052	A752THV	1083	B83WUL	1150	B150WUL	1329	C329BUV	1414	C414BUV
1058	B58WUL	1111	B111WUL	1151	B151WUL	1330	C330BUV		
1059	B59WUL	1113	B113WUL	1153	B153WUL	1331	C331BUV		

MC1	P481HEG	Marshall Midibus	Marshall	B29F	1996	
MC345	N715FLN	Mercedes-Benz 814D	Cacciamali Ibis	C20F	1995	Ex R&I, 1996
MC346	N716FLN	Mercedes-Benz 814D	Cacciamali Ibis	C20F	1995	Ex R&I, 1996
MC347	N717FLN	Mercedes-Benz 814D	Cacciamali Ibis	C20F	1995	Ex R&I, 1996

MM254–268   MAN 11.220   Marshall   B38F   1996   Ex R&I, 1996

254	N121XEG	257	N124XEG	260	N127XEG	263	N130XEG	266	N133XEG
255	N122XEG	258	N125XEG	261	N128XEG	264	N131XEG	267	N134XEG
256	N123XEG	259	N126XEG	262	N129XEG	265	N132XEG	268	N135XEG

MMS269   N161YEG   Mercedes-Benz 811D   Marshall   B26F   1996

MM270–278   MAN 11.220   Marshall   B38F   1996

270	P470JEG	272	P472JEG	274	P474JEG	276	P476JEG	278	P478JEG
271	P471JEG	273	P473JEG	275	P475JEG	277	P477JEG		

MRL210–222   Optare MetroRider MR03   Optare   B26F   1991–93   Ex London Buses, 1994

210	J210BWU	213	J213BWU	216	J216BWU	219	J219BWU	222	K422HWY
211	J211BWU	214	J214BWU	217	J217BWU	220	J220BWU		
212	J212BWU	215	J215BWU	218	J218BWU	221	J221BWU		

MV249–253   MAN 11.190   Optare Vecta   B42F   1995   Ex R&I, 1996

249	M507ALP	250	M508ALP	251	N701FLN	252	N702FLN	253	N703FLN

MW18–37   Mercedes-Benz 811D   Wright   B26F   1993   Ex London Buses, 1994

18	NDZ7918	22	NDZ7922	26	NDZ7926	30	NDZ7930	34	NDZ7934
19	NDZ7919	23	NDZ7923	27	NDZ7927	31	NDZ7931	35	NDZ7935
20	NDZ7920	24	NDZ7924	28	NDZ7928	32	NDZ7932	36	K510FYN
21	NDZ7921	25	NDZ7925	29	NDZ7927	33	NDZ7933	37	K476FYN

O77	C945FMJ	Ford Transit 190	Chassis Developments	12	1985	Ex R&I, 1996
O87	F87GGC	Mercedes-Benz 811D	Robin Hood	C29F	1989	Ex R&I, 1996
O90	F90GGC	Mercedes-Benz 811D	Robin Hood	C29F	1989	Ex R&I, 1996
OM67	ULL897	Mercedes-Benz 811D	Optare StarRider	C29F	1988	Ex R&I, 1996
OM93	165BXP	Mercedes-Benz 811D	Optare StarRider	C29F	1991	Ex R&I, 1996
OM243	M501ALP	Optare MetroRider MR33	Optare	B25F	1995	Ex R&I, 1996
OM244	M502ALP	Optare MetroRider MR33	Optare	B25F	1995	Ex R&I, 1996
OM279	P509NWU	Optare MetroRider	Optare	B25F	1996	

RM29–2186   AEC Routemaster 5RM   Park Royal   H36/28R   1959–65   Ex London Buses, 1994
*RM1081, RM2097 ex London Transport Buses, 1997

29	OYM453A	1081	81CLT	1348	348CLT	1840	840DYE	2136	CUV136C
268	VLT268	1158	158CLT	1568	568CLT	1971	ALD971B	2153	CUV153C
446	WLT446	1171	171CLT	1700	KGJ167A	1979	ALD979B	2186	CUV186C
646	KFF257	1185	XYJ427	1758	758DYE	2023	ALM23B		
765	WLT765	1218	218CLT	1799	799DYE	2041	ALM41B		
912	WLT912	1283	283CLT	1804	EYY327B	2097	ALM97B		

RML903–2731 AEC Routemaster 7RM   Park Royal   H40/32R   1961–67   Ex London Buses, 1994

903	WLT903	2296	CUV296C	2395	JJD395D	2511	JJD511D	2679	SMK679F
2282	CUV282C	2310	CUV310C	2413	JJD413D	2561	JJD561D	2699	SMK699F
2284	CUV284C	2367	JJD367D	2419	JJD419D	2603	NML603E	2731	SMK731F
2295	CUV295C	2393	JJD393D	2479	JJD479D	2620	NML620E		

S11–20   Scania N113DRB   Alexander RH   H47/31F   1991   Ex London Buses, 1994

11	J811HMC	13	J813HMC	15	J815HMC	17	J817HMC	19	J819HMC
12	J812HMC	14	J814HMC	16	J816HMC	18	J818HMC	20	J820HMC

S81	RIB6197	Kässbohrer Setra S210HI	Kässbohrer Optimal	C26FT	1989	Ex R&I, 1996
S82	RIB6198	Kässbohrer Setra S210HI	Kässbohrer Optimal	C26FT	1989	Ex R&I, 1996
S83	RIB6199	Kässbohrer Setra S210HI	Kässbohrer Optimal	C26FT	1989	Ex R&I, 1996

SR108–121   Mercedes-Benz 811D   Optare StarRider   B26F   1989   Ex London Buses, 1994

108	G108KUB	111	G111KUB	114	G114KUB	117	G117KUB	121	G121KUB
109	G109KUB	112	G112KUB	115	G115KUB	118	G118KUB		
110	G110KUB	113	G113KUB	116	G116KUB	120	G120KUB		

T82–221   Leyland Titan TNLXB2RRSp   Park Royal   H44/26D*   1979/80   * T126 is H44/24D
Ex London Suburban, 1995

82	CUL82V	111	CUL111V	202	CUL202V
97	CUL97V	126	CUL126V	205	CUL205V
102	CUL102V	141	CUL141V	221	CUL221V

T251	GYE251W	Leyland Titan TNLXB2RR	Park Royal/Leyland	H44/26D	1981	Ex London Suburban, 1995
T405	KYV405X	Leyland Titan TNLXB2RR	Leyland	H44/24D	1982	Ex London Suburban, 1995
T423	KYV423X	Leyland Titan TNLXB2RR	Leyland	H44/24D	1982	Ex London Suburban, 1995
TC10	N781SJU	Toyota Coaster HZB50R	Caetano Optimo II	C18F	1996	Ex R&I, 1996
TC11	N782SJU	Toyota Coaster HZB50R	Caetano Optimo II	C18F	1996	Ex R&I, 1996
VH1	804DYE	Volvo B10M–60	Van Hool Alizée H	C49FT	1988	Ex R&I, 1996
VH2	NJI9479	DAF MB230DKFL615	Van Hool Alizée H	C49FT	1987	Ex R&I, 1996
VH3	G260EHD	DAF MB230LT615	Van Hool Alizée H	C49FT	1989	Ex R&I, 1996
VH4	HIL6975	Volvo B10M–61	Van Hool Alizée H	C49FT	1986	Ex R&I, 1996

VH5–9   Volvo B10M–62   Van Hool Alizée HE   C48FT   1996   VH6 ex R&I, 1996

5	N655EWJ	6	N656EWJ	7	N657EWJ	8	N658EWJ	9	N659EWJ

VP330–341   Volvo B10M–60   Plaxton Paramount 3500 3   C49FT*   1990/91   * VP334 is C53F
Ex R&I, 1996

330	SVO89	334	RIB5084	337	RIB7017	341	OO1942
333	43FJF	336	RIB5086	338	RIB7018		

201–217   Volvo Olympian YN2RV18Z4   Northern Counties Palatine II H47/25D 1993–94 Ex London Suburban, 1995

201	L201SKD	205	L205SKD	209	L209SKD	214	L214TWM
202	L202SKD	206	L206SKD	210	L210SKD	215	L215TWM
203	L203SKD	207	L207SKD	212	L212TWM	216	L216TWM
204	L204SKD	208	L208SKD	213	L213TWM	217	L217TWM

303	D85DOT	Mercedes-Benz 609D	Robin Hood	C14F	1987	Ex R&I, 1996
539	H539YCX	DAF SB220LC550	Ikarus Citibus	B50F	1991	Ex R&I, 1996
848	F848YJX	DAF SB220LC550	Optare Delta	B49F	1989	Ex Merseybus, 1996
849	F849YJX	DAF SB220LC550	Optare Delta	DP48F	1989	Ex R&I, 1996
901	D733JJD	Kässbohrer Setra S215HR	Kässbohrer Rational	C49FT	1987	Ex R&I, 1996

Previous registrations

D733JJD	D396BPE, RIB6195	OYM453A	VLT29	RIB7017	G77RGG	XYJ427	185CLT
EYY327B	804DYE	RIB4315	F504YNV, A17AML	RIB7018	G78RGG	165BXP	J361BNW
G122CLD	G210LGK,RIB5087	RIB4316	F206HGN	RIB6199	F83GGC	804DYE	F967GMW
HIL6975	C29VJF	RIB5082	F202HGN	RIB7002	CWN12A, H403HOY	43FJF	G43RGG
K476FYN	NDZ7937	RIB5083	F203HGN	RIB5086	G86RGG	33LUG	J823GGF
K510FYN	NDZ7936	RIB5084	G74RGG	RIB6197	F81GGC		
KFF257	WLT646	RIB5085	K415MGN	RIB8431	L416PAR		
KGJ167A	700DYE	RIB6198	F82GGC	RIB8432	F91JGJ		
NJI9479	D276YCX	RIB7003	F207HGN	SVO89	G44RGG		
OO1942	H608UWR	RIB7004	G208LGK	ULL897	E200UWT		

Special liveries
Sightseers livery: M1045/67, M1393/6 and all single-deck coaches.
X43 Express: S11/3-20
Contract Liveries: 077/87/90, IR203/6/7

NETWORK WATFORD

LDT Ltd, Castle Street, Luton, LU1 3AJ

LDT Ltd, known as "The Shires", was formed from the former London Country North West and Luton & District fleets, and adopted its present trading name in April 1995, together with local marketing identities. Compared with the size of the company, the London Transport element of its operations is small.

London Country North West gained an involvement in LT minibus work in 1986, though this ceased in 1988. Subsequently, routes 142 and 340 were gained and allocated to Watford garage. The green and grey privatisation livery was changed to blue and yellow with grey skirt when operations were relaunched in April 1995. Watford operations, previously known as Watfordwide and from 1993 Watford Bus, were marketed as "Network Watford" from this date. Route 142 is currently the subject of retendering.

In addition, Network Watford work route 350 with LT agreement, and other local services in and around Watford, both commercial and on behalf of Hertfordshire County Council. The depot is at St Albans Road, Garston.

LR85 is one of fifteen Leyland bodied Leyland Olympians delivered new in 1991 and used continuously from The Shires' Garston garage at Watford. August 1996 finds the bus at Stanmore on route 142 in the livery inherited from its days with Luton & District. At the beginning of 1997, this livery was still very much in the majority on the two LT contract routes. Capital Transport

Network Watford also operate route 340 between Edgware and Harrow. LR52, one of the Roe-bodied examples freshly-painted into the new Company livery of blue and yellow, belies its 1984 vintage as it passes through Wealdstone in September 1996.
Capital Transport

NETWORK WATFORD

Route 142 and 340 Buses

LR49–55		Leyland Olympian ONTL11/1R		Roe		H43/29F	1984	Ex London Country North West, 1990
LR49	A149FPG	**LR52**	A152FPG	**LR54**	A154FPG			
LR51	A151FPG	**LR53**	A153FPG	**LR55**	A155FPG			

LR70	B270LPH	Leyland Olympian ONTL11/1R		Eastern Coach Works		H43/29F	1985	Ex London Country North West, 1990
LR71	B271LPH	Leyland Olympian ONTL11/1R		Eastern Coach Works		H43/29F	1985	Ex London Country North West, 1990
LR72	B272LPH	Leyland Olympian ONTL11/1R		Eastern Coach Works		H43/29F	1985	Ex London Country North West, 1990
LR73	B273LPH	Leyland Olympian ONTL11/1R		Eastern Coach Works		H43/29F	1985	Ex London Country North West, 1990

LR81–95		Leyland Olympian ONCL10/1RZ		Leyland		H47/31F	1989/90	Ex London Country North West, 1990
LR81	G281UMJ	**LR84**	G284UMJ	**LR87**	G287UMJ	**LR90**	G290UMJ	**LR93** G293UMJ
LR82	G282UMJ	**LR85**	G285UMJ	**LR88**	G288UMJ	**LR91**	G291UMJ	**LR94** G294UMJ
LR83	G283UMJ	**LR86**	G286UMJ	**LR89**	G289UMJ	**LR92**	G292UMJ	**LR95** G295UMJ

LR96–102		Leyland Olympian 0N2R50C13Z4		Leyland		H47/29F	1991	
LR96	H196GRO	**LR98**	H198GRO	**LR100**	H201GRO	**LR102**	H203GRO	
LR97	H197GRO	**LR99**	H199GRO	**LR101**	H202GRO			

SOVEREIGN

London Sovereign Ltd, Station Road, Borehamwood, Herts, WD6 1HB
Sovereign Buses (Harrow) Ltd, Babbage Road, Stevenage, Herts, SG1 2EQ

Sovereign Bus & Coach was established in January 1989 as the eastern part of the former London Country North East. Now forming part of the Blazefield Group, the Company has two separate divisions employed on LT work: Sovereign Harrow and London Sovereign, the latter being the former fleet of BTS, Borehamwood.

The Harrow operation was set up in December 1990 for locally-based LT contracts gained at that time. Borehamwood Travel Services was formed with twenty vehicles from the fleet of C J Franklin of Borehamwood in August 1984. BTS ran an emergency service on LT route 292 during the London Country North East strike of January 1988 and took over the route formally from February 1988 until it was lost on tender from November 1993. Before losing this route, the Company gained the contract to operate crew route 13 (Golders Green to Aldwych) using 22 RMLs leased from London Buses. This route remained unique as being the sole London service operated daily with Routemasters until the summer of 1996, when the Sunday operation was converted to one-person operation. Blazefield Holdings, the owners of Sovereign, acquired BTS in August 1994 and the trading name was changed from BTS to London Sovereign in September 1996, although only the word Sovereign appears on the vehicles.

LT routes operated are 13, 114, 606 (London Sovereign), H10, H11, H13, H17 (Sovereign Harrow). London Sovereign also operate Hertfordshire County Council route 861.

The London Sovereign fleet is in poppy red livery with yellow relief and housed at Station Road, Borehamwood. The Harrow fleet is in blue and cream and housed at Pinner Road, Harrow.

Route 114 was originally won on tender by BTS of Borehamwood but, together with its base, vehicles and route 13, these were bought by Sovereign. Former BTS Leyland Olympian L143 is seen in South Harrow. Capital Transport

Sovereign's five Titans are used alongside the Olympians on route 114. T706 is seen on the Sunday operation of route 13, which derives its vehicles from the 114 allocation.
Malc McDonald

LONDON SOVEREIGN

L139–152 Leyland Olympian ON2R50C13Z4   Northern Counties   H47/30F   1991

L139	H139GGS	**L142**	H142GGS	**L145**	H145GGS	**L148**	H148GGS	**L151**	H151GGS
L140	H140GGS	**L143**	H143GGS	**L146**	H146GGS	**L149**	H149GGS	**L152**	H152GGS
L141	H141GGS	**L144**	H144GGS	**L147**	H147GGS	**L150**	H150GGS		

RML2265–2756 AEC Routemaster R2RH/1   Park Royal   H40/32R   1965–68 On loan from London Buses; Cummins engines

RML2265	CUV265C	**RML2487**	JJD487D	**RML2582**	JJD582D	**RML2663**	SMK663F	**RML2719**	SMK719F
RML2322	CUV322C	**RML2527**	JJD527D	**RML2598**	JJD598D	**RML2668**	SMK668F	**RML2756**	SMK756F
RML2341	CUV341C	**RML2538**	JJD538D	**RML2627**	NML627E	**RML2674**	SMK674F		
RML2404	JJD404D	**RML2563**	JJD563D	**RML2633**	NML633E	**RML2686**	SMK686F		
RML2443	JJD443D	**RML2569**	JJD569D	**RML2659**	SMK659F	**RML2694**	SMK694F		

T57	WYV57T	Leyland Titan TNLXB2RRSP	Park Royal	H44/28F	1979	Ex London Buses, 1994
T277	GYE277W	Leyland Titan TNLXB2RR	Leyland	H44/28F	1981	Ex London Buses, 1992
T620	NUW620Y	Leyland Titan TNLXB2RR	Leyland	H44/28F	1982	Ex London Buses, 1993
T706	OHV706Y	Leyland Titan TNLXB2RR	Leyland	H44/28F	1983	Ex London Buses, 1993
T777	OHV777Y	Leyland Titan TNLXB2RR	Leyland	H44/28F	1983	Ex London Buses, 1992

SOVEREIGN (Harrow)

409–424   Mercedes-Benz 811D   Reeve Burgess Beaver   B31F   1990–91

409	H409FGS	**413**	H413FGS	**418**	H418FGS	**422**	H422FGS
410	H410FGS	**415**	H415FGS	**419**	H419FGS	**423**	H423FGS
411	H411FGS	**417**	H417FGS	**421**	H421FGS	**424**	H424FGS

435   K5SBC   Mercedes-Benz 811D   Plaxton Beaver   B31F   1993

455–461   Mercedes-Benz 811D   Plaxton Beaver   B31F   1995

455	M455UUR	**457**	M457UUR	**459**	M459UUR	**461**	M461UUR
456	M456UUR	**458**	M458UUR	**460**	M460UUR		

907–931   Mercedes-Benz 709D   Reeve Burgess Beaver   B23F   1989/90

907	G907UPP	**922**	H922FGS	**926**	H926FGS	**930**	H930FGS
914	G914UPP	**923**	H923FGS	**927**	H927FGS	**931**	H931FGS
921	H921FGS	**925**	H925FGS	**929**	H929FGS		

In late 1996, the London Sovereign Routemasters on loan from London Buses for route 13 gained new logos. October 1996 finds RML2756, numerically the newest RML in the fleet, turning into Pall Mall East displaying the new Sovereign logo. Colin Lloyd

The entire Sovereign (Harrow) operation is undertaken using either Mercedes-Benz 709D or 811D buses with Reeve Burgess Beaver or its successor, the Plaxton Beaver body. Representing the Plaxton Beaver type mounted on the Mercedes-Benz 811D is 455 in South Harrow on route H10 in August 1996. The notice above the front wheel refers to the Smartcard ticket system. Capital Transport

STAGECOACH EAST LONDON

East London Bus & Coach Co Ltd, 2–4 Clements Road, Ilford, Essex, IG1 1BA

East London was purchased by the Stagecoach Group on 6th September 1994, taking 595 vehicles. Major fleet updating is now in hand; all but one of the originally acquired Metroriders have gone, and significant inroads to the fleet of Leyland Titans are now starting.

Vehicles began to lose their white relief stripes and grey skirts very quickly, both through full and partial repaints, and to gain Stagecoach East London logos. From the end of 1994 Routemasters appeared with cream relief bands instead of white, and gold Stagecoach East London logos.

Having taken over responsibility for Stagecoach Selkent private hire work in addition to their own, Stagecoach East London promptly converted two Titans to coach seating in the autumn of 1994, outshopping them in a smart East London Coaches livery. Subsequently both vehicles received undated registrations from RMLs. A handful of vehicles, both owned and loaned, have carried corporate Stagecoach livery and have been so used outside the inner London area.

The fleet operates from garages at Barking, Bow, Leyton, Romford, Stratford and Upton Park. Stratford vehicles are maintained at Bow.

Two of East London's Leyland Titans have received corporate Stagecoach livery, and are thereby debarred from use on central routes. T282, photographed in May 1996, could at first glance well pass for one of the many Titans now in service with other Stagecoach subsidiaries. Tony Wilson

Forty Scania N113s with Northern Counties bodywork were delivered to East London garages in 1991/2. S66 was found at North Woolwich. After a period during which the type has been concentrated at Upton Park, some have been moved to Leyton. Martin Ruthe

1996 saw the arrival of forty-three Volvo Olympians with Northern Counties bodywork, with more expected during 1997. The first twenty-six have single-door bodywork for use on outer suburban routes, as shown by VN1 at Harold Hill. Martin Ruthe

The last of twenty-seven Dennis Darts with Alexander Dash bodywork to standard Stagecoach specification, DAL27 stands in Ilford in October 1996 showing the continued use of Hoppa branding for some East London routes.
Colin Lloyd

STAGECOACH EAST LONDON

DA10–35 DAF SB220LC550 Optare Delta B40D+31* 1989–93 * DA10 is DP36D+39
Ex London Buses, 1994

10	G684KNW	16	J716CYG	22	J722CYG	28	J728CYG	34	K634HWX
11	J711CYG	17	J717CYG	23	J723CYG	29	J729CYG	35	K635HWX
12	J712CYG	18	J718CYG	24	J724CYG	30	K630HWX		
13	472YMF	19	J719CYG	25	J725CYG	31	K631HWX		
14	J714CYG	20	J720CYG	26	J726CYG	32	K632HWX		
15	YLJ332	21	J721CYG	27	J727CYG	33	K633HWX		

DA13/5 are on extended loan to Stagecoach South (Hampshire Bus)

DAL1–27 Dennis Dart 9.8SDL3054 Alexander Dash B36F 1995

1	N301AMC	7	N307AMC	13	N313AMC	19	N319AMC	25	N325AMC
2	N302AMC	8	N308AMC	14	N314AMC	20	N320AMC	26	N326AMC
3	N303AMC	9	N309AMC	15	N315AMC	21	N321AMC	27	N327AMC
4	N304AMC	10	N310AMC	16	N316AMC	22	N322AMC		
5	N305AMC	11	N311AMC	17	N317AMC	23	N323AMC		
6	N306AMC	12	N312AMC	18	N318AMC	24	N324AMC		

DRL109–146 Dennis Dart 9SDL3024 Plaxton Pointer B34F+16 1993 * DRL139–146 are 9SDL3034
Ex London Buses, 1994

109	K109SRH	117	K117SRH	125	K125SRH	133	K133SRH	141	L141VRH
110	K110SRH	118	K118SRH	126	K126SRH	134	K134SRH	142	L142VRH
111	K211SRH	119	K119SRH	127	K127SRH	135	K135SRH	143	L143VRH
112	K112SRH	120	K120SRH	128	K128SRH	136	L136VRH	144	L144VRH
113	K113SRH	121	K121SRH	129	K129SRH	137	L137VRH	145	L145VRH
114	K114SRH	122	K122SRH	130	K130SRH	138	L138VRH	146	L146VRH
115	K115SRH	123	K123SRH	131	K131SRH	139	L139VRH		
116	K116SRH	124	K124SRH	132	K132SRH	140	L140VRH		

DW133–159 Dennis Dart 8.5SDL3015 Wright Handybus B29F+16 1993 Ex London Buses, 1994

133	NDZ3133	139	NDZ3139	145	NDZ3145	151	NDZ3151	157	NDZ3157
134	NDZ3134	140	NDZ3140	146	NDZ3146	152	NDZ3152	158	NDZ3158
135	NDZ3135	141	NDZ3141	147	NDZ3147	153	NDZ3153	159	NDZ3159
136	NDZ3136	142	NDZ3142	148	NDZ3148	154	NDZ3154		
137	NDZ3137	143	NDZ3143	149	NDZ3149	155	NDZ3155		
138	NDZ3138	144	NDZ3144	150	NDZ3150	156	NDZ3156		

DWL15–26 Dennis Dart 9SDL3016 Wright Handybus B35F+17 1993 Ex London Buses, 1994

15	NDZ3015	18	NDZ3018	21	NDZ3021	24	NDZ3024
16	NDZ3016	19	NDZ3019	22	NDZ3022	25	NDZ3025
17	NDZ3017	20	NDZ3020	23	NDZ3023	26	NDZ3026

The gold-based Stagecoach fleetname is carried to good effect on East London's refurbished RMLs, as represented by RML2639 at Aldgate Station in July 1996. All but one of East London's RMLs now carry cream relief. Mike Harris

Still carrying a traditional underlined London Transport fleetname, and with the original type of front ventilator grille and offside route number indicator, RM613 could well have been photographed as new were it not for the Dayglo destination blinds. In fact it was caught in Pall Mall in July 1995. Colin Lloyd

Two of the former BEA front-entrance Routemasters remain in service with East London. RMA5, caught in Pall Mall near the Athenaeum Club in April 1996, still carries the original type of trafficator. M.E. Lyons

Freshly-repainted in a red version of traditional Green Line Livery, RMC1485 (with incomplete fleet number transfers) stands at Paddington in August 1996 on route 15, on which it still makes cameo appearances. Note the Routemaster lettering applied above the fleet number for all East London Routemasters. Geoff Rixon

LA1–16   Dennis Lance 11SDA3101   Alexander PS   B39D   1992   Ex Selkent, 1995

1	J101WSC	5	J105WSC	10	J110WSC	14	J114WSC
3	J103WSC	7	J107WSC	11	J411WSC	16	J116WSC
4	J104WSC	9	J109WSC	13	J113WSC		

LCY1–7   Dennis Dart SLF   Alexander ALX200   B29DL   1997   London City Airport blue livery

1	P801NGN	3	P803NGN	5	P805NGN	7	P807NGN
2	P802NGN	4	P804NGN	6	P806NGN		

MR16	D476PON	MCW Metrorider MF150/14	Metro-Cammell-Weymann	B23F	1987 Ex London Buses, 1994
MRL144	H144UUA	Optare MetroRider MR03	Optare	B26F	1990 Ex Selkent, 1996
RM613	WLT613	AEC Routemaster 5RM	Park Royal	H36/28R	1960 Ex London Buses, 1994
RM980	USK625	AEC Routemaster 5RM	Park Royal	H36/28R	1961 Ex Bluebird Buses, 1997
RM1289u	XSL596A	AEC Routemaster 5RM	Park Royal	H36/28R	1962 Ex Bluebird Buses, 1997
RM1527	527CLT	AEC Routemaster 5RM	Park Royal	H36/28R	1963 Ex London Buses, 1994
RM1599u	YTS820A	AEC Routemaster 5RM	Park Royal	H36/28R	1963 Ex Bluebird Buses, 1997
RMA5	NMY635E	AEC Routemaster 9RM	Park Royal	H35/25F	1967 Ex London Buses, 1994
RMA8	NMY640E	AEC Routemaster 9RM	Park Royal	H32/24F	1967 Ex London Buses, 1994
RMC1456	LFF875	AEC Routemaster 6RM	Park Royal	H32/25RD	1962 Ex London Buses, 1994
RMC1461	461CLT	AEC Routemaster 6RM	Park Royal	H32/25RD	1962 Ex London Buses, 1994
RMC1485	485CLT	AEC Routemaster 6RM	Park Royal	H32/25RD	1962 Ex London Buses, 1994

RML886–2760   AEC Routemaster 7RM   Park Royal   H40/32R   1961–68   Iveco engines except a AEC and c Cummins Ex London Buses, 1994

886c	WLT886	2415	JJD415D	2481	JJD481D	2607	NML607E	2671c	SMK671F
890c	XFF814	2429	JJD429D	2488	JJD488D	2610c	NML610E	2696c	SMK696F
898	XFF813	2435	JJD435D	2493	JJD493D	2616c	NML616E	2705c	SMK705F
2272c	CUV272C	2437	JJD437D	2495c	JJD495D	2624	NML624E	2709	SMK709F
2286c	CUV286C	2444	JJD444D	2496c	JJD496D	2639c	NML639E	2723c	SMK723F
2300	CUV300C	2445c	JJD445D	2497c	JJD497D	2641c	NML641E	2738	SMK738F
2303	CUV303C	2450	JJD450D	2541c	JJD541D	2642c	NML642E	2743c	SMK743F
2311c	CUV311C	2451	JJD451D	2550c	JJD550D	2657	NML657E	2748c	SMK748F
2392	JJD392D	2456c	JJD456D	2565c	JJD565D	2661c	SMK661F	2749	SMK749F
2399	JJD399D	2462	JJD462D	2581c	JJD581D	2665	SMK665F	2760a	SMK760F
2402	JJD402D	2470	JJD470D	2592	JJD592D	2670c	SMK670F		

S22–29   Scania N113DRB   Alexander RH   H47/31F   1991   Ex London Buses, 1994

22	J822HMC	24	J824HMC	26	J826HMC	28	J828HMC
23	J823HMC	25	J825HMC	27	J827HMC	29	J829HMC

S30–71   Scania N113DRB   Northern Counties Countybus Palatine   H44/25D   1991/92   * S30/1 are H47/33F Ex London Buses, 1994

30	J230XKY	39	J139HMT	48	K848LMK	57	K857LMK	66	K866LMK
31	J231XKY	40	J140HMT	49	K849LMK	58	K858LMK	67	K867LMK
32	J132HMT	41	J141HMT	50	K850LMK	59	K859LMK	68	K868LMK
33	J133HMT	42	J142HMT	51	K851LMK	60	K860LMK	69	K869LMK
34	J134HMT	43	J143HMT	52	K852LMK	61	K861LMK	70	K870LMK
35	J135HMT	44	J144HMT	53	K853LMK	62	K862LMK	71	K871LMK
36	J136HMT	45	J145HMT	54	K854LMK	63	K863LMK		
37	J137HMT	46	K846LMK	55	K855LMK	64	K864LMK		
38	J138HMT	47	K847LMK	56	K856LMK	65	K865LMK		

SLD1–9   Dennis Dart SFD212BR1TGW1   Alexander ALX200   B36F   1996

1	P21HMF	3	P23HMF	5	P25HMF	7	P27HMF	9	P29HMF
2	P31HMF	4	P24HMF	6	P26HMF	8	P28HMF		

SLD10-19   Dennis Dart SLF   Alexander ALX200   B36F   1997

10	12	14	16	18
11	13	15	17	19

SLW15–30   Scania N113CRL   Wright Pathfinder 320   B37D   1994   SLW15 ex London Buses, 1994

15	RDZ6115	19	RDZ6119	23	RDZ6123	27	RDZ6127
16	RDZ6116	20	RDZ6120	24	RDZ6124	28	RDZ6128
17	RDZ6117	21	RDZ6121	25	RDZ6125	29	RDZ6129
18	RDZ6118	22	RDZ6122	26	RDZ6126	30	RDZ6130

SP2   K302FYG   DAF DB250WB505   Optare Spectra   H44/23D   1992   Ex London Buses, 1994

SR1–119   Mercedes-Benz 811D   Optare StarRider   B26F   1988–89   Ex London Buses, 1994

1	E155CGJ	50	F50CWY	70	F170FWY	75	F175FWY	105	G105KUB
2	E712LYU	56	F156FWY	71	F171FWY	76	F176FWY	106	G106KUB
12	F912YWY	60	F160FWY	72	F172FWY	78	F178FWY	107	G107KUB
13	F913YWY	65	F165FWY	73	F173FWY	79	F179FWY	119	G119KUB
32	F32CWY	66	F166FWY	74	F174FWY	91	G91KUB		

T1–163   Leyland Titan TNLXB2RRSp   Park Royal   H44/26D   1978–80   a H44/22D b H44/26F
c DPH44/26F
Ex London Buses, 1994 (T163 ex Selkent, 1995)

1a	THX401S	11	WYV11T	21a	WYV21T	31a	WYV31T	63c	WLT890
2	THX402S	12	WYV12T	22	WYV22T	32a	WYV32T	80c	WLT898
3	WYV3T	13a	WYV13T	23a	WYV23T	33	WYV33T	163	CUL163V
4a	WYV4T	14a	WYV14T	24a	WYV24T	34a	WYV34T		
6a	WYV6T	15a	WYV15T	25	WYV25T	35a	WYV35T		
7a	WYV7T	16a	WYV16T	28a	WYV28T	36	WYV36T		
8a	WYV8T	18a	WYV18T	30	WYV30T	39	WYV39T		

T261   GYE261W   Leyland Titan TNTL112RR   Park Royal/Leyland   H44/26D   1981   Ex London Buses 1994

T264–789   Leyland Titan TNLXB2RR   Leyland   H44/24D   1981–83   a H44/26D b O44/24D
Ex London Buses, 1994
(T282 ex Selkent, 1995)

264	GYE264W	467	KYV467X	543	KYV543X	591	NUW591Y	647	NUW647Y
266a	GYE266W	469	KYV469X	544	KYV544X	592	NUW592Y	648	NUW648Y
268	GYE268W	470	KYV470X	545	KYV545X	593	NUW593Y	649	NUW649Y
272	GYE272W	471	KYV471X	546	KYV546X	595	NUW595Y	650	NUW650Y
282a	KYN282X	473	KYV473X	548	KYV548X	597	NUW597Y	651	NUW651Y
285a	KYN285X	476	KYV476X	549	KYV549X	598	NUW598Y	652	NUW652Y
286	KYN286X	480	KYV480X	550	NUW550Y	600	NUW600Y	653t	NUW653Y
298	KYN298X	486	KYV486X	551	NUW551Y	601	NUW601Y	654	NUW654Y
306	KYN306X	488	KYV488X	552	NUW552Y	602	NUW602Y	657	NUW657Y
311a	KYV311X	490	KYV490X	553	NUW553Y	603	NUW603Y	658	NUW658Y
318	KYV318X	492	KYV492X	554	NUW554Y	604	NUW604Y	659	NUW659Y
320a	KYV320X	495	KYV495X	555	NUW555Y	605	NUW605Y	660	NUW660Y
326	KYV326X	496	KYV496X	556	NUW556Y	606	NUW606Y	662	NUW662Y
331a	KYV331X	497	KYV497X	557	NUW557Y	608	NUW608Y	663	NUW663Y
334	KYV334X	498	KYV498X	558	NUW558Y	609	NUW609Y	664	NUW664Y
340	KYV340X	500	KYV500X	559	NUW559Y	610	NUW610Y	665	NUW665Y
360	KYV360X	501	KYV501X	560	NUW560Y	613	NUW613Y	666	NUW666Y
366	KYV366X	502	KYV502X	562	NUW562Y	614	NUW614Y	668	NUW668Y
378	KYV378X	503	KYV503X	563	NUW563Y	615	NUW615Y	669	NUW669Y
379	KYV379X	504	KYV504X	564	NUW564Y	617	NUW617Y	670	NUW670Y
380	KYV380X	505	KYV505X	565	NUW565Y	619	NUW619Y	671	NUW671Y
386	KYV386X	506	KYV506X	566	NUW566Y	621	NUW621Y	672	NUW672Y
387	KYV387X	508	KYV508X	568	NUW568Y	622	NUW622Y	673	NUW673Y
394	KYV394X	512bt	KYV512X	569	NUW569Y	623	NUW623Y	675	NUW675Y
395	KYV395X	513	KYV513X	571	NUW571Y	624	NUW624Y	686	OHV686Y
406	KYV406X	514	KYV514X	572	NUW572Y	625	NUW625Y	688	OHV688Y
428	KYV428X	515	KYV515X	573	NUW573Y	626	NUW626Y	691	OHV691Y
434	KYV434X	517	KYV517X	574	NUW574Y	627	NUW627Y	697	OHV697Y
437	KYV437X	521	KYV521X	575	NUW575Y	629	NUW629Y	699	OHV699Y
439	KYV439X	522	KYV522X	576	NUW576Y	630	NUW630Y	702	OHV702Y
441	KYV441X	525	KYV525X	577	NUW577Y	631t	NUW631Y	719	OHV719Y
444	KYV444X	526	KYV526X	578	NUW578Y	632	NUW632Y	724	OHV724Y
445	KYV445X	527	KYV527X	579	NUW579Y	633	NUW633Y	729	OHV729Y
446	KYV446X	529	KYV529X	580	NUW580Y	634	NUW634Y	731	OHV731Y
448	KYV448X	531	KYV531X	581	NUW581Y	636	NUW636Y	738	OHV738Y
453	KYV453X	532	KYV532X	582	NUW582Y	637	NUW637Y	743	OHV743Y
454	KYV454X	533	KYV533X	583	NUW583Y	639	NUW639Y	744	OHV744Y
456	KYV456X	535	KYV535X	584	NUW584Y	640	NUW640Y	749	OHV749Y
458	KYV458X	536	KYV536X	585	NUW585Y	641	NUW641Y	751	OHV751Y
460	KYV460X	537	KYV537X	586	NUW586Y	642	NUW642Y	759	OHV759Y
461	KYV461X	539	KYV539X	587	NUW587Y	643	NUW643Y	761	OHV761Y
462	KYV462X	540	KYV540X	588	NUW588Y	644	NUW644Y	769	OHV769Y
465	KYV465X	541	KYV541X	589	NUW589Y	645	NUW645Y	784	OHV784Y
466	KYV466X	542	KYV542X	590	NUW590Y	646	NUW646Y	789	OHV789Y

During 1995, Selkent's entire batch of sixteen Dennis Lances built in 1992 with Alexander bodywork moved north of the Thames to East London. LA3, newly-repainted into all-red livery, was caught in Ilford. The type is now being withdrawn for transfer elsewhere. Tony Wilson

DA12 is one of twenty Optare Deltas delivered to East London in 1992, and was photographed in Ilford lacking nearside fleetname. Tony Wilson

The first examples of Alexander ALX bodywork in London are provided by nine low-floor Dennis Darts delivered to East London. SLD4 shows off this new design in Faraday Avenue, Walthamstow. Russell Upcraft

East London continue to operate a number of Optare StarRiders from their Stratford base. SR71 was caught south of the Thames at Surrey Quays in June 1996 prior to returning through the Rotherhithe tunnel. Colin Brown

T802–1050 — Leyland Titan TNLXB2RR · Leyland · H44/26D · 1983–84 · Ex London Buses, 1994

802	OHV802Y	840	A840SUL	902	A902SYE	944	A944SYE	965t	A965SYE
819	RYK819Y	846	A846SUL	905	A905SYE	945	A945SYE	971t	A971SYE
826	A826SUL	849	A849SUL	921	A921SYE	949t	A949SYE	1022	A622THV
827	A827SUL	867	A867SUL	922	A922SYE	953t	A953SYE	1026	A626THV
832	A832SUL	873	A873SUL	935	A935SYE	960t	A960SYE	1050	A650THV

T1128	630DYE	Leyland Titan TNLXB1RF	Park Royal	DPH43/29F	1979	Ex London Buses, 1994

VN1–43 — Volvo Olympian · Northern Counties Palatine 1 · H49/25D* · 1996 · * VN1–26 are H49/31F

1	P801GMU	10	P810GMU	19	P819GMU	28	P528HMP	37	P537HMP
2	P802GMU	11	P811GMU	20	P820GMU	29	P529HMP	38	P538HMP
3	P803GMU	12	P812GMU	21	P821GMU	30	P530HMP	39	P539HMP
4	P804GMU	13	P813GMU	22	P822GMU	31	P531HMP	40	P540HMP
5	P805GMU	14	P814GMU	23	P823GMU	32	P532HMP	41	P541HMP
6	P806GMU	15	P815GMU	24	P824GMU	33	P533HMP	42	P542HMP
7	P807GMU	16	P816GMU	25	P825GMU	34	P534HMP	43	P543HMP
8	P808GMU	17	P817GMU	26	P826GMU	35	P535HMP		
9	P809GMU	18	P818GMU	27	P527HMP	36	P536HMP		

VP4	H654UWR	Volvo B10M–60	Plaxton Paramount 3500 3	C49FT	1991	Ex Willetts, Yorkley, 1995
VP5	H655UWR	Volvo B10M–60	Plaxton Paramount 3500 3	C49FT	1991	Ex Wallace Arnold, 1995
VP7	H657UWR	Volvo B10M–60	Plaxton Paramount 3500 3	C49FT	1991	Ex Metrobus, Orpington, 1995
1716	NFX667	Dennis Dart 9.8SDL3017	Alexander AM	DP32F	1992	Ex Busways, 1996;
						on extended loan to Stagecoach South (Hampshire Bus)
1719	XYK976	Dennis Dart 9.8SDL3017	Alexander AM	DP32F	1992	Ex Busways, 1996;
						on extended loan to Stagecoach South (Hants & Surrey)

Previous registrations

E155CGJ	E711LYU, WLT461	USK625	WLT980	XYK976	K719PCN
H654UWR	H659UWR	WLT890	WYV63T	YLJ332	J715CYG
H655UWR	H660UWR	WLT898	CUL80V	YTS820A	599CLT
H657UWR	H655UWR	XFF813	WLT898	630DYE	WDA3T, 486CLT
LFF875	456CLT	XFF814	WLT890	472YMF	J713CYG
NFX667	K716PCN	XSL591A	289CLT		

On order
50 Volvo Olympians with Alexander bodywork

Named vehicles
RMA5 *King Charles*, RMC 1456 *Prince Albert*, RMC 1461 *Sir Christopher Wren*, RMC1485 *King William I*, T512 *Phoenix*, T1128 *The Ranger*

Special liveries
East London Line livery: SR12/3/32/50/6/60/70/2–6/91/105–7/19.
Green Line livery: RMC1461.
Stagecoach livery: T3, T282.
Tesco livery: DW159.
South West Trains livery: DA13/5, 1716/9.
London City Airport: LCY1–7

STAGECOACH SELKENT

South East London & Kent Bus Co Ltd, 180 Bromley Road, London SE26 2XA

Selkent was purchased by the Stagecoach group on 6th September 1994, taking 414 vehicles. Selkent was the only major LBL subsidiary to have achieved all-opo by the date of privatisation.

Vehicles began to lose their white relief stripes and grey skirts very quickly, both through full and partial repaints, and to gain Stagecoach Selkent logos. Dedicated trainers carry corporate Stagecoach livery. The private hire operation was wound up during October 1994 and the coaching fleet, including three coach-seated Titans, was dispersed to other Stagecoach companies. Subsequent adverse tendering results have led to some contraction in the fleet, with significant quantities of Leyland Titans passing to other companies in the Stagecoach group, though in the autumn of 1996 a number of Titans were transferred in from East London for newly-gained route P3.

The fleet operates from garages at Bromley, Catford and Plumstead.

Selkent have released many of their earlier Leyland Titans to other Stagecoach subsidiaries as a result of fleet renewal and contract losses. T1007 survived as one of the newer examples at the beginning of 1997, though its withdrawal was imminent. It was found at Surrey Quays in June 1996. Colin Brown

Many of the large order for Leyland Olympians received by London Buses in the mid-1980s found their way to Plumstead garage. L23 was found on a short working of route 53 in October 1996. This route is now more normally the province of newer Olympians. Stephen Madden

Bodied by Alexander, fifty-two Volvo Olympians joined the Selkent fleet in 1995 and were allocated to Plumstead for use on route 53. No.352, the last of the batch, passes the diplomatic offices in Whitehall in August 1996. Geoff Rixon

Shortly before privatisation in 1994, Selkent received twelve Dennis Lances with Plaxton Verde bodywork, all of which were put into use on route 208. LV9 had recently received Stagecoach corporate London livery when photographed at Orpington in June 1996. Colin Lloyd

As with East London, Selkent have since received quantities of standard Stagecoach single-deckers. No.606 is one of thirty-nine Dennis Darts with Alexander bodywork received during the past year, and is depicted at Greenwich in June 1996. Colin Lloyd

STAGECOACH SELKENT

DT28–55 — Dennis Dart 8.5SDL3003 — Carlyle Dartline — B28F* — 1990 — * DT28–31 are DP28F / Ex London Buses, 1994

28	49CLT	32	VLT240	35	G35TGW	38	G38TGW	55a	WLT575
30	G30TGW	33	G33TGW	36	G36TGW	39	G39TGW		
31	G31TGW	34	G34TGW	37	G37TGW	40	G40TGW		

DW59–71 — Dennis Dart 8.5SDL3003 — Wright Handybus — B28F — 1991 — Ex London Buses, 1994

59	JDZ2359	61	JDZ2361	63	JDZ2363	65	JDZ2365
60	JDZ2360	62	JDZ2362	64	JDZ2364	71	JDZ2371

L7–263 — Leyland Olympian ONLXB/1RH — Eastern Coach Works — H42/26D* — 1986–87 — * L260–3 are DPH42/26D / Ex London Buses, 1994

7	C807BYY	54	C54CHM	80	C80CHM	110	C110CHM	129	D129FYM
9	C809BYY	55	C55CHM	81	C81CHM	111	C111CHM	130	D130FYM
10	C810BYY	57	C57CHM	82	C82CHM	112	C112CHM	131	D131FYM
11	C811BYY	60	C60CHM	83	C83CHM	114	C114CHM	132	D132FYM
12	C812BYY	61	C61CHM	86	C86CHM	115	C115CHM	133	D133FYM
15	C815BYY	62	C62CHM	87	C87CHM	116	C116CHM	134	D134FYM
18	C818BYY	64	C64CHM	91	WLT491	117	C117CHM	136	D136FYM
19	C819BYY	67	C67CHM	92	C92CHM	118	C118CHM	137	D137FYM
23	C23CHM	68	C68CHM	94	C94CHM	119	C119CHM	141	D141FYM
28	C28CHM	69	C69CHM	97	C97CHM	120	C120CHM	142	D142FYM
29	C29CHM	70	C70CHM	98	C98CHM	121	C121CHM	144	D144FYM
30	C30CHM	71	C71CHM	103	C103CHM	122	C122CHM	145	D145FYM
42	C42CHM	72	C72CHM	104	C104CHM	123	D123FYM	260	VLT20
43	C43CHM	73	C73CHM	105	C105CHM	124	D124FYM	262	VLT14
44	C44CHM	74	C74CHM	106	C106CHM	125	D125FYM	263	D367JJD
48	C48CHM	75	C75CHM	107	C107CHM	126	D126FYM		
51	C51CHM	76	C76CHM	108	C108CHM	127	D127FYM		
53	C53CHM	77	C77CHM	109	C109CHM	128	D128FYM		

LV1–12 — Dennis Lance 11SDA3108 — Plaxton Verde — B42D — 1994 — Ex London Buses, 1994

1	L201YAG	4	L204YAG	7	L207YAG	10	L210YAG
2	L202YAG	5	L205YAG	8	L208YAG	11	L211YAG
3	L203YAG	6	L206YAG	9	L209YAG	12	WLT461

MRL141–176 — Optare MetroRider MR03 — Optare — B26F — 1990–91 — Ex London Buses, 1994

141u	H141UUA	148	H148UUA	154	H154UUA	165	H165WWT	171	H171WWT
142	H142UUA	149	H149UUA	160	H160WWT	166	H166WWT	172	H172WWT
143	H143UUA	150	H150UUA	161	H161WWT	167	H167WWT	173	H173WWT
145	H145UUA	151	H151UUA	162	H162WWT	168	H168WWT	174	H174WWT
146u	H146UUA	152	H152UUA	163	H163WWT	169	H169WWT	175	H175WWT
147	H147UUA	153	H153UUA	164	H564WWR	170	H170WWT	176	H176WWT

MT4	F394DHL	Mercedes-Benz 709D	Reeve Burgess Beaver	B23F	1988	Ex London Buses, 1994
MW2	HDZ2602	Mercedes-Benz 811D	Wright	B19FL	1989	Ex London Buses, 1994
MW8	HDZ2608	Mercedes-Benz 811D	Wright	B19FL	1989	Ex London Buses, 1994
MW14	HDZ2614	Mercedes-Benz 811D	Wright	B19FL	1989	Ex London Buses, 1994

T9–230 — Leyland Titan TNLXB2RRSp — Park Royal — H44/26D* — 1979/80 — Ex East London, 1996 — * T17, T37/8 are H44/22D; T230 is H44/24D

9	WYV9T	20	WYV20T	40	WYV40T	193	CUL193V	230	EYE230V
10	WYV10T	26	WYV26T	66	WYV66T	214	CUL214V		
17	WYV17T	37	WYV37T	140	CUL140V	222	CUL222V		
19	WYV19T	38	WYV38T	175	CUL175V	223	CUL223V		

T260	GYE260W	Leyland Titan TNLXB2RR	Park Royal/Leyland	H44/26D	1981	Ex East London, 1996
T262	GYE262W	Leyland Titan TNLXB2RR	Park Royal/Leyland	H44/26D	1981	Ex East London, 1996
T263	GYE263W	Leyland Titan TNLXB2RR	Park Royal/Leyland	H44/26D	1981	Ex East London, 1996

T267–797 — Leyland Titan TNLXB2RR — Leyland — H44/24D — 1981–83 — a H44/26D / Ex London Buses, 1994

267a	GYE267W	455	KYV455X	721	OHV721Y	770	OHV770Y	785	OHV785Y
368	KYV368X	616	NUW616Y	740	OHV740Y	771	OHV771Y	791	OHV791Y
447	KYV447X	680	OHV680Y	748	OHV748Y	772	OHV772Y	797	OHV797Y

804	OHV804Y	843	A843SUL	918	A918SYE	1032	A632THV	1099	B99WUV
805	OHV805Y	845	A845SUL	925	A925SYE	1034	A634THV	1100	B100WUV
810	OHV810Y	847	A847SUL	926	A926SYE	1035	A635THV	1101	B101WUV
812	OHV812Y	848	A848SUL	950	A950SYE	1036	A636THV	1103	B103WUV
813	OHV813Y	850	A850SUL	951	A951SYE	1045	A645THV	1106	B106WUV
814	OHV814Y	854	A854SUL	961	A961SYE	1048	A648THV	1108	B108WUV
815	OHV815Y	855	A855SUL	976	A976SYE	1052	A652THV	1110	B110WUV
816	RYK816Y	856	A856SUL	978	A978SYE	1065	A65THX	1112	B112WUV
818	RYK818Y	857	A857SUL	988	A988SYE	1067	A67THX *	1113	B113WUV
821	RYK821Y	858	A858SUL	996	A996SYE	1077	A77THX	1114	B114WUV
822	RYK822Y	859	A859SUL	999	A999SYE	1079	B79WUV	1115	B115WUV
828	A828SUL	866	A866SUL	1003	A603THV	1081	B81WUV	1116	B116WUV
829	A829SUL	868	A868SUL	1007	A607THV	1083	B83WUV	1117	B117WUV
830	A830SUL	874	A874SUL	1013	A613THV	1084	B84WUV	1118	B118WUV
834	A834SUL	877*	A877SUL	1025	A625THV	1089	B89WUV	1119	B119WUV
836	A836SUL	880*	A880SUL	1027	A627THV	1091	B91WUV	1121	B121WUV
837	A837SUL	881†	A881SUL	1028	A628THV	1092	B92WUV	1122	B122WUV
838	A838SUL	882†	A882SUL	1029	A629THV	1093	B93WUV	1124	B124WUV
841	A841SUL	883†	A883SUL	1030	A630THV	1096	B96WUV	1125	B125WUV
842	A842SUL	885†	A885SUL	1031	A631THV	1097	B97WUV		

301–352 Volvo Olympian YN2RC16V3 Northern Counties Palatine H45/23D 1995

301	M301DGP	312	M312DGP	323	N323HGK	334	N334HGK	345	N345HGK
302	M302DGP	313	M313DGP	324	N324HGK	335	N335HGK	346	N346HGK
303	M303DGP	314	M314DGP	325	N325HGK	336	N336HGK	347	N347HGK
304	M304DGP	315	M315DGP	326	N326HGK	337	N337HGK	348	N348HGK
305	M305DGP	316	M316DGP	327	N327HGK	338	N338HGK	349	N349HGK
306	M306DGP	317	M317DGP	328	N328HGK	339	N339HGK	350	N350HGK
307	M307DGP	318	M318DGP	329	N329HGK	340	N340HGK	351	N351HGK
308	M308DGP	319	M319DGP	330	N330HGK	341	N341HGK	352	N352HGK
309	M309DGP	320	M320DGP	331	N331HGK	342	N342HGK		
310	M310DGP	321	N321HGK	332	N332HGK	343	N343HGK		
311	M311DGP	322	N322HGK	333	N353HGK	344	N344HGK		

601–614 Dennis Dart 9.8SDL3054 Alexander Dash B36F 1995/96

601	N601KGF	604	N604KGF	607	N607KGF	610	N610KGF	613	N613LGC
602	N602KGF	605	N605KGF	608	N608KGF	611	N611LGC	614	N614LGC
603	N603KGF	606	N606KGF	609	N609KGF	612	N612LGC		

615–640 Dennis Dart 9.8m Alexander Dash B36F 1996

615	P615PGP	620	P620PGP	625	P625PGP	630	P630PGP	636	P636PGP
616	P616PGP	621	P621PGP	626	P626PGP	631	P631PGP	637	P637PGP
617	P617PGP	622	P622PGP	627	P627PGP	632	P632PGP	638	P638PGP
618	P618PGP	623	P623PGP	628	P628PGP	633	P633PGP	639	P639PGP
619	P619PGP	624	P624PGP	629	P629PGP	634	P634PGP	640	P640PGP

3001–3008 Leyland Titan TNLXB2RRSp Park Royal H44/24D* 1979/80 Ex London Buses, 1994
*3002/5/6/8 are H44/26D

3001t	CUL137V	3003t	CUL114V	3005t	CUL86V	3007t	CUL120V
3002t	CUL98V	3004t	CUL224V	3006t	CUL142V	3008t	CUL130V

Previous registrations

D367JJD	D263FUL, VLT9	VLT240	G32TGW	WLT575	G55TGW
VLT14	D262FUL	WLT461	L212YAG	49CLT	G28TGW
VLT20	D260FYM	WLT491	C91CHM		

Named vehicles
L260 *Renown*, L262 *Invincible*, L263 *Conqueror*, LV12 *Enterprise*

On order
29 Volvo Olympians with Northern Counties bodywork

With a registration thirty-one years older than its present bearer, DT32 is one of the second batch of Dennis Darts ordered by LBL in the early days of the type, and carries Carlyle bodywork with a front end which was rebuilt following major accident damage. It was photographed at Eltham in September 1996. Mike Harris

Selkent's minibus operations were updated with an infusion of stretched Optare MetroRiders at the turn of the decade. MRL151 was found on route 380 in Lewisham Road in June 1996. Mike Harris

Eight of these Wright bodied Darts inherited from London Buses are in the Stagecoach Selkent fleet, later Darts having Alexander bodywork – a firm favourite with the group. DW63 is seen at Lewisham. Laurie Rufus

The sixteen original Mercedes-Benz 811D vehicles with Wright bodywork are now reduced to three which are used chiefly on mobility bus services with Selkent. MW14 cruises south through Bromley town centre. Colin Lloyd

TELLINGS-GOLDEN MILLER

Tellings-Golden Miller Ltd, 20A, Wintersells Road, Byfleet, Surrey, KT14 7LF

In June 1985, Tellings Coaches of Byfleet took control of the stage carriage operations of Golden Miller of Feltham. Five Bristol RE buses were purchased to operate the four routes, but these were soon sold. Two of the routes were transferred in October 1987 to Fountain Coaches, which operated from the former Golden Miller premises. The remaining two routes, the 602 (Feltham to Shepperton) and the 606 (Staines to Stanwell Moor), were retained, and the businesses of Tellings Coaches and Golden Miller were merged. The new company gained the contracts to run LT routes 116 and 117 from Brentford to Staines, but these were taken over by London & Country from 23rd February 1992.

The company gained their latest LT tendered route with the acquisition of new route S3 between Belmont and Worcester Park from April 1995. Three new Plaxton Beaver-bodied Mercedes-Benz 811Ds were purchased for this contract. Routes 513 and 740 are also operated. Fleet livery is blue and white, and vehicles are garaged at Wintersells Road, Byfleet.

TELLINGS-GOLDEN MILLER

Bus Fleet

E224PWY	MCW MetroRider MF150/34	MCW	DP23F	1987	Ex Cardiff Bluebird, Grangetown, 1994
E232PWY	MCW MetroRider MF150/41	MCW	DP23F	1987	Ex Cardiff Bluebird, Grangetown, 1995
E804UDT	MCW MetroRider MF150/15	MCW	B23F	1987	Ex Stevensons, Uttoxeter, 1994
E808UDT	MCW MetroRider MF150/15	MCW	B23F	1987	Ex Cardiff Bluebird, Grangetown, 1994
E604VKC	MCW MetroRider MF150/40	MCW	DP23F	1987	Ex Cardiff Bluebird, Grangetown, 1995
F101YVP	MCW MetroRider MF150/115	MCW	B25F	1988	Ex Cardiff Bluebird, Grangetown, 1995
M70TGM	Mercedes-Benz 709D	Plaxton Beaver	B23F	1995	
M80TGM	Mercedes-Benz 709D	Plaxton Beaver	B23F	1995	
M90TGM	Mercedes-Benz 709D	Plaxton Beaver	B23F	1995	
N70TGM	Mercedes-Benz 609D	Plaxton Beaver	B23F	1996	

The coach fleet is listed in the London Coach Handbook.

Crossing a picturesque Hampton Court Bridge is Tellings Golden Miller N70TGM, the newest vehicle in the bus fleet. New in 1996, it is a Plaxton Beaver bodied Mercedes-Benz 709D. May 1996 finds the bus having left Kingston on Surrey County Council route 513 to Downside near Cobham. Geoff Rixon

THAMESWAY

Essex Buses Ltd, Stapleford Close, New Writtle Street, Chelmsford, Essex, CM2 0SD

In July 1990 the LT routes and other western operations of Eastern National passed to the new Thamesway company, since when the LT operations have expanded. This has resulted in the arrival of many new Mercedes-Benz minibuses, together with a substantial intake of Dennis Darts. From 1st December 1995, the Company was re-united with Eastern National to become Essex Buses Ltd, but both retain their individual names. LT routes operated are 191, 193, 214, 362, 379, 389, 399, 462, D8, W9, W11, W12, W13, 950-956, 958, 959, 961.

THAMESWAY (LT contract vehicles)

230	D230PPU	Mercedes-Benz L608D	Reeve Burgess	B20F	1986	Ex Eastern National, 1990
231	D231PPU	Mercedes-Benz L608D	Reeve Burgess	B20F	1986	Ex Eastern National, 1990
233	D233PPU	Mercedes-Benz L608D	Reeve Burgess	B20F	1986	Ex Eastern National, 1990
234	D234PPU	Mercedes-Benz L608D	Reeve Burgess	B20F	1986	Ex Eastern National, 1990

245–260
Mercedes-Benz 709D   Reeve Burgess Beaver   B23F   1989

245	F245MVW	249	F249NJN	252	F252NJN	255	F255RHK	258	F258RHK
246	F246MVW	250	F250NJN	253	F253RHK	256	F256RHK	259	F259RHK
247	F247NJN	251	F251NJN	254	F254RHK	257	F257RHK	260	F260RHK
248	F248NJN								

261	D764KWT	Mercedes-Benz 609D	Robin Hood	B20F	1987	Ex SWT, 1994

301–306
Mercedes-Benz 709D   Reeve Burgess Beaver   B23F   1990

301	H301LPU	303	H303LPU	304	H304LPU	305	H305LPU	306	H306LPU
302	H302LPU								

388–395
Mercedes-Benz 709D   Reeve Burgess Beaver   B20F   1991   Ex Eastern National, 1992

388	H388MAR	390	H390MAR	392	H392MAR	394	H394MAR	395	H395MAR
389	H389MAR	391	H391MAR	393	H393MAR				

396	K396GHJ	Mercedes-Benz 709D	Plaxton Beaver	B23F	1993
397	K397GHJ	Mercedes-Benz 709D	Plaxton Beaver	B23F	1993
398	K398GHJ	Mercedes-Benz 709D	Plaxton Beaver	B23F	1993

401-410
Mercedes-Benz 711D   Plaxton Beaver   B23F   1996

401	P401HPU	403	P403HPU	405	P405HPU	407	P407HPU	409	P409HPU
402	P402HPU	404	P404HPU	406	P406HPU	408	P408HPU	410	P410HPU

800–804
Mercedes-Benz 811D   Reeve Burgess Beaver   B31F   1989

800	F800RHK	801	F801RHK	802	F802RHK	803	F803RHK	804	F804RHK

805–811
Mercedes-Benz 811D   Plaxton Beaver   B31F   1992

805	K805DJN	807	K807DJN	809	K809DJN	811	K811DJN
806	K806DJN	808	K808DJN	810	K810DJN		

851	N851CPU	Dennis Dart 9.5SDL3053	Marshall C36	B17FL	1995
852	N852CPU	Dennis Dart 9.5SDL3053	Marshall C36	B17FL	1995
853	N853CPU	Dennis Dart 9.5SDL3053	Marshall C36	B17FL	1995
854	N854CPU	Dennis Dart 9.5SDL3053	Marshall C36	B17FL	1995

901–917
Dennis Dart 9SDL3016   Plaxton Pointer   B35F   1992

901	K901CVW	905	K905CVW	909	K909CVW	913	K913CVW	917	K917CVW
902	K902CVW	906	K906CVW	910	K910CVW	914	K914CVW		
903	K903CVW	907	K907CVW	911	K911CVW	915	K915CVW		
904	K904CVW	908	K908CVW	912	K912CVW	916	K916CVW		

973–987
Dennis Dart SFD412BR5TGD1   Plaxton Pointer   B40F   1996

973	N973EHJ	976	N976EHJ	979	N979EHJ	982	N982EHJ	985	N985EHJ
974	N974EHJ	977	N977EHJ	980	N980EHJ	983	N983EHJ	986	N986EHJ
975	N975EHJ	978	N978EHJ	981	N981EHJ	984	N984EHJ	987	N987EHJ

Thamesway operate route 462 with four of these 20 seat Mercedes-Benz 608Ds, now the oldest buses in use on London routes by the company. Still in old livery, 233 passes the Sainsbury's supermarket in Ilford in September 1995. Tony Wilson

The latest Dennis Darts in the Thamesway fleet are fifteen examples bought in 1996 for newly won tendered route 191. Ponders End in June 1996 sees 987 arriving from Brimsdown Station. Capital Transport